Also by Leo Heaps

Escape from Arnhem
Rebel in the House
The High Rise
Log of the Centurion
The Grey Goose of Arnhem
The Quebec Plot
Operation Morning Flight

Hugh Hambleton,
SPY

Hugh Hambleton, SPY

Thirty Years with the KGB

LEO HEAPS

⬒ METHUEN

Toronto   New York   London   Sydney   Auckland

Canadian Cataloguing in Publication Data
Heaps, Leo, 1923–
Hugh Hambleton, spy

ISBN 0-458-96970-2

1. Hambleton, Hugh.   2. Spies—Canada—Biography.
3. Espionage, Russian.   I. Title.

UB271.R92H36 1983   327.1′2′0924   C83-099012-7

Printed and bound in United States of America
1 2   3   4   5   83   88 87 86 85 84

- CONTENTS -

– INTRODUCTION –

The sources of information for this book are all primary. They come from many original documents: the subject himself, Professor Hugh George Hambleton; a former official associated with the Mossad, the Israeli secret service; and a valuable member of a security service in one of the countries where Professor Hambleton operated for the Soviet espionage organization, the KGB. Long personal knowledge of the Hambleton family accounts for a considerable portion of the material.

There has been much fiction written on this subject and much ignorance shown of the deep penetration by the Soviets into the fabric of Canadian life. Neither the government nor the people have been aware of the depth of subversion by the KGB in Canada, nor have they been able to cope with it. We have been easy pickings, the back door into the United States, the KGB's most important adversary. In high places in government and private and public life, there are people whose background and beliefs make them prime targets for subversion, a subversion done so subtly and skilfully that the victim is unaware that he is being cultivated, compromised, until he is part of the Soviet spy network.

That is how liberties are first eroded and nations jeopardized. Long before he may be of use, the Russians carefully pick their man. One day, they hope the victim will rise to a position of influence in Western society. When that happens it is already too late. This is the story of such a man.

PART ONE

Hugo

- CHAPTER ONE -

The Interview

JANUARY 1980

The phone rang late on a Sunday evening.

I put down my book and glanced wearily at my watch. It was five minutes after eleven. I lay in bed, wondering who would be calling at that hour of the night. I was tired and debated whether to answer. The phone persisted in ringing, suggesting a kind of perseverance that belonged to an intelligent being who refused to give up until I responded. Reluctantly I picked up the instrument.

"Mr. Heaps?"

I thought I recognized the male caller, but I wasn't sure.

"Who is this?" I asked.

"Are you Leo Heaps?" the voice repeated.

"Yes, who are you?"

The caller ignored me. Instead I could hear him conferring with someone else, but his remarks were not intelligible.

"We'd like to talk to you as soon as possible about an important matter." The caller's voice assumed an impersonal authority.

I was sure I was being subjected to a practical joke. And I played along.

"Phone me in the morning when I'm more awake," I suggested. "And at least tell me your name so I know whom I'm speaking with."

My wife, half asleep and curious about what was happening, turned to me and opened her eyes. "Who's phoning you at this time of night?"

2

I put my hand over the mouthpiece. "One of those crazy calls. A practical joker."

"Then it must be one of *your* friends," she said. "I can't think of anyone who would want to phone at this hour on a Sunday. Hang up and take the phone off the hook," she said irritably.

"Good-bye," I said to the caller upon instructions. "It was nice of you to have phoned." I hung up, but I didn't take the phone off the hook. I never like to deliberately stop the phone from ringing, since I do receive important calls from countries in far parts of the world. Less than a minute later, to my annoyance, the phone rang again.

"Okay," I said, picking up the receiver, "if you characters continue to bother me, I'll have to call the police. Or if it's you, Harold, and you've had a little too much to drink, please, do me a favour and call someone else."

"This *is* the police. The RCMP. We would like to talk to you as soon as possible."

It was now almost eleven-thirty. Did the RCMP call people at that time?

"Why would the RCMP want to see me?" I had become a little more cautious.

Once again I heard a second, more distant voice conferring.

"We can't tell you over the phone. Can we meet tomorrow morning? We're willing to fly in from Ottawa and see you at your home."

"I want your names and phone numbers, and I'll call you back."

"We'll give you our names tomorrow," the voice answered obstinately. "But we'll give you a number to call. You can verify what we've just told you by mentioning your name."

"One moment." I was growing more than a little impatient. "I'm not going to do anything or see anyone until you tell me what you want."

Once again I could hear my caller engaging in a muffled conversation with an associate.

"We want to talk to you about a matter of national security."

"Espionage?"

I must have spoken the word quite loudly. My wife unwrapped the sheet from her head and sat up in bed.

"What did you just say?" she asked.

"The RCMP are phoning me about espionage."

"What have you been up to, Leo?" she asked, quite serious.

One of those lightning-like visions of total recall which is supposed to be the last act of the dying flashed through my mind. From all the adventures of my life I tried to visualize some incident involving spies or intelligence since World War II. I could think of none.

"Are you absolutely sure you have the right person?" I asked.

"Yes, it's you we want to talk to," the caller insisted.

My wife interrupted, "What have you been doing on those European trips?"

I calmed Tamar. She had become noticeably nervous, and I couldn't blame her. No doubt there was a simple explanation, but I didn't know what it was. I assured her that in this computer age mix-ups could easily occur, but she was not satisfied.

"Look," I said to the caller. "You have my name, surely you can tell me yours." There was a moment of hesitation, and then he said, "McIlroy." And he gave me his telephone number.

"I'll check you out," I said. "Do you mind?"

"Hell, no." And he hung up.

I dialed the number in Ottawa. It was a central switchboard for the RCMP.

"Do you have a McIlroy there?" I requested.

"Yes, sir. Do you want me to get him?" the operator answered.

"No, don't bother." I hung up.

"Can't we phone someone in Ottawa to protest?" my wife asked. "Maybe our phone has been tapped for months. Who knows what crazy things have been going on."

The incident had long since ceased to amuse me, if indeed there had been anything amusing to start with. I phoned McIlroy and told him I would be in Ottawa in two days and could meet him at RCMP headquarters. I would call on arrival and arrange a convenient time.

I switched on my tape recorder while the conversation was still fresh in my mind and recorded what had happened.

RCMP headquarters in Ottawa on Metcalf Street are housed in a large, multi-storey brick building with an impressive glass entrance. Beyond the doors, behind a bruised wooden counter sits an RCMP guard in shirt and tie. Like other government buildings in Ottawa this one has the same characterless quality, the same grey sterility that seems to be the fate of all such structures.

Three days went by before I arrived in the early evening to keep my strange appointment with the security service of the RCMP. I had taken the precaution of informing a member of

Parliament friend about the odd, late-night phone calls at my home and the mysterious rendezvous. The MP knew me well and was as mystified as I about the reason, but we both felt further inquiries would serve no useful purpose. At the interview I would listen with interest to my interrogators and discover why I had been summoned.

I entered the building, gave my name to the constable at the desk, and said I was expected. I was told to wait in the lobby: someone would shortly come down for me. The polished floor tiles smelled of antiseptic, a sterile cleanliness. The walls were bare, the furniture sparse and government issue. A door opened and shut on the floor above, and the sound echoed down to me. But I could hear no footsteps, although I knew many of the rooms were occupied. People worked here throughout the night. The elevators were busy.

I wondered whether somewhere in one of the rooms a dossier existed on myself, and I concluded this was most likely. I had always championed causes where people's liberty was at stake, but I could not recall ever having engaged in any subversive activity. Here I was, a Canadian, summoned by the security service without explanation. What rights did I have? True, I could choose not to come, but these men would seek me out wherever I might be. Soon these faceless RCMP investigators would appear, and they would ask their questions. Would I have to defend myself? And if so, against whom and what? The fear of the unknown magnified itself as I sat alone in the empty corridor waiting for what seemed an unnecessarily long time.

Fifteen minutes passed. I smiled at the absurdity of my anxiety. The constable at the desk smiled back. I had now been waiting twenty minutes. An elevator descended. It stopped on the ground floor, the door opened, and two plainclothes men stepped out and walked in my direction, unsmiling. I didn't particularly like the strained look of neutrality on either of their faces. The small man with a shock of red hair led the way, stopped and uttered my name. Both men then removed their wallets, flashing their identification. The first man introduced himself as Inspector Frank Pratt, and his larger companion identified himself as Sergeant Robert McIlroy.

"Would you follow us?" Pratt asked politely.

I followed without a word. The elevator took us to the third floor. Then I was conducted through a deserted corridor of closed doors to a large room furnished with a long government-issue varnished boardroom table surrounded by a number of office chairs. I took my place at one end of the table while Pratt sat at the other and McIlroy took a place in between. Neither man carried a notebook, nor did it appear they intended to record our conversation. They were sitting waiting for me, I thought, to begin talking. But I had nothing to say.

Maybe a minute or two elapsed. I noticed both officials had their coats draped over a chair. In the corner a wet umbrella leaned against the cream-coloured wall. It had started raining that evening just before I arrived. That meant whoever owned the still-wet umbrella had probably come about the same time I had. For a second or two longer I regarded my would-be inquisitors. The leading question, I anticipated, would come from Inspector Pratt. He was in charge. He possessed the more aggressive demeanour of the two men and would not encourage confidence in a stranger, certainly not in me. He might be a deadly foe if he sensed advantage or had cornered an adversary, but I had the feeling from the beginning that he didn't quite know how to deal with me. He was carefully sizing me up in the silence. His partner, McIlroy, had a sizeable paunch, a soft face, grey hair, and the drooping, bleary eyes of a basset hound. An unhealthy pallor was superimposed on the veined blue skin of the fleshy cheeks and throat. He gave the impression of being the softer of the two, but I concluded that his quiet manner was an affectation, designed to deceive. They were two people to be careful with.

"Well," I said at last, "what is this all about?"

Pratt answered my question with one of his own: "Do you know Hugh Hambleton?"

"I have known him most of my life," I answered. "Is that why you brought me here?"

I had not seen Hugo for several years, not since he had provided material for a book I had written on a fictional revolt in Quebec. If the meeting was only about Hugo, I already felt better.

McIlroy joined in the conversation. "Do you read the newspapers?"

"No," I said, "I haven't been paying particular attention to the news lately."

"If you had," McIlroy responded, "you would have read that your friend Hambleton has been spying for the Soviet Union."

I looked at both men in turn with some incredulity. Obviously there was a genuine expression of disbelief on my face.

"Are you sure we are talking about the same man?"

"He has been under investigation for several years. He has admitted spying for the Soviets."

"He has?" I said numbly.

"You know him well, don't you?" Pratt re-entered the conversation.

Racing through my mind was the possibility that I might have been under clandestine investigation for many months. My phone could easily have been tapped. I have friends whose conversations, to say the least, might have sounded highly compromising. I had one acquaintance who always started his conversation with a Russian greeting, which I never understood. He claimed to be a relative of the Czar.

But underneath it all, any apprehension I had anticipated at this meeting magically disappeared at the mention of the name of my old friend. The idea of Hugo Hambleton being an important Soviet spy was too absurd for me to believe. I could not visualize him as a secret agent. He would be sure to throw the entire Russian system into chaos. He would never undertake a role so ambitious except in the wildest flights of his imagination. What secrets did he have to give away? I couldn't think of any. He might go to great lengths to stand out from his fellow man, but surely he would not go that far. Certainly there was no one less suited to live under the cruel dictatorship of communism. He was a lonely eccentric and had been one for the lifetime I had known him.

A few minutes passed. My hosts were staring at me uncomfortably, staring at the smug smile I wore on my face. Did they want me to say something helpful? I had difficulty accepting the idea that there could be a serious discussion on the subject of Hugo being a Russian spy. Finally, I said, "If Hugo is the best the Russians can come up with, Canada is safe."

Neither man cracked a smile. Pratt's face hardened. McIlroy's drooping eyes enlarged slightly.

"You know Delameter in Paris?" Pratt asked. "He's one of Hambleton's friends."

"I've heard of him, but I never met him."

"When did you see Hambleton last, and where?" McIlroy asked. He was in no hurry. He was the friendly one.

"A few years ago in Quebec City. I stayed with him in his apartment in St. Foy. Before that we met in Ottawa occasionally. I think that's all the recent meetings I recall." Later I remembered that he had stayed in my flat in London after the Quebec visit.

"You saw him in Haiti six years ago," Pratt said.

That was true. I had seen him in Haiti. They were obviously looking for some link between us. A Soviet connection? Preposterous.

"Lili Galeva," Pratt said, "have you met his Yugoslavian friend?"

"The one who is so sick," I answered. "Hugo told me about her." McIlroy nodded, encouraging me to continue without comment. I repeated the story Hugo had told me about his Yugoslavian girlfriend, whom he intended to marry. She had been invited to Canada on a number of occasions. The news of her illness had saddened me, but I never paid much attention to his female companions.

Behind Hugo were two broken marriages, three children and a constantly chaotic personal lifestyle. My interrogators listened in silence to the story, but I think they already knew it. After several seconds McIlroy spoke: "Hugh told you this, did he?"

"Yes. Has she died?"

McIlroy and Pratt ignored my remark and displayed no feeling for the apparent tragedy. Two policemen, I thought, two detectives with a few homely refinements that transformed them into anti-espionage agents. Pratt still retained his air of subdued aggression as McIlroy played the appeaser. I did not doubt that they knew a lot more than they told me. There were too many knowing nods. This act was too planned, too rehearsed. They had been through this many times before. A team of fine actors who had carefully done their homework and knew what questions to ask, what weaknesses to exploit.

"Could it be," I said at last, "that you have made a mistake?"

McIlroy smiled wisely, "He's made a written confession. He told us of meetings with Russian agents in Quebec, drops for documents mapped out in the woods outside Montreal. We found coded messages and secret documents among his papers. He has bank accounts in foreign countries that would come from only one source. We visited his cottage in the woods, twenty-five miles outside Montreal. The place was abandoned, windows broken, doors off their hinges. The forest reaches right up to the front verandah. We turned it inside out."

"What did you find?" I asked.

"We can't tell you," McIlroy said.

Pratt said, "When you went to Hungary with Hambleton in 1956, did he go for the same reason as yourself?"

That year I had headed a mission for the International Rescue Committee, which operated along the Austro-Hungarian border. That part was true. But I had not gone beyond the

Hungarian border, nor had I been with Hugo. At that point in my life I had not seen him for many years. I was beginning to take a dislike to the inspector. "If anyone told you I went to Hungary with Hambleton I would suggest you take a long, careful look at them."

"I heard you might have," Pratt corrected without an apology, but with less enthusiasm. McIlroy added no comment. I had hoped Pratt had given up trying to associate me with the Russians, but he wasn't the kind of man who ever gave up.

"Did you meet Hambleton in Paris in 1961?" Pratt asked.

"In Paris—I never met him in Paris. I saw him on his occasional trips back to Ottawa and in London, where I lived for fifteen years."

"You saw him at his mother's home on Ruskin, in Ottawa?" McIlroy added. "You know his mother?"

I admitted I knew her well. I had known her all my life. She was a powerful, dominant woman, the unquestioned matriarch of the family. She was now ninety-two years old and, with the exception of being deaf and recovering from a broken hip, was as impressive an intellect as she had been when I first met her.

"You know Josephine, Hugo's sister?" McIlroy questioned.

I nodded affirmatively, noticing that McIlroy referred to Hambleton by his usual first name. I learned later that after two years of regular interrogation they had become friends, with that peculiar relationship that binds the hunter and the hunted.

"I'm still not convinced that Hugo is the spy you think he is," I said with less conviction.

"We have all the evidence we need," McIlroy said, "and more. He has worked for the Russians for a long time. All the proof is now in the hands of the solicitor general. We are waiting for the government to decide whether or not to prosecute."

"I'm afraid I can't help you further," I said.

"Anything that you can recall would be helpful," Pratt appealed. "Anything. His family, his home, his sister, mother, father."

"You seem to know almost everything. What can I add?"

"I don't think you are telling us everything," Pratt said.

I had a reluctance to pour out all I had known about Hugo; what I knew about the man didn't concern the security service. If he had had a secret life, I had not known about it.

"Aside from his reputed contact with the Soviets, the maps and documents you found, what did Hugo hand over to the Russians? What information of importance did he pass?" I asked.

"What more do you need than an admission?" McIlroy replied.

"He was named as an important Russian agent," Pratt added.

"By whom?"

"A KGB colonel who was caught and turned."

"I'm skeptical about Soviet agents who turn," I said obstinately. But the security service obviously had evidence—more than they cared to disclose.

So Hugo had really done it, I said to myself. Was it actually conceivable? I had known him well in his youth, and we had met regularly over the years. But one can't always keep up with the changing personalities of once good friends. The years may change people, but certain basic qualities remain the same throughout one's life. And Hugo was someone whom I felt had really never grown up. Did I really not know Hugh Hambleton? Was everything he had said and done calculated to deliberately mislead and deceive his friends? The idea bordered on the fantastic, but then I had always believed Hugo's personality to be composed of one part fantasy. McIlroy's voice startled me.

"We offered him protection against the Russians," McIlroy went on. "But he refused to accept it. He said he didn't need any."

"Hugo is either the supreme master of deception," I said, "or this is a Canadian fuck-up of monumental proportions."

I rose. As far as I was concerned the interview was over. I had said everything I had to say. My interrogators rose with me. We took the elevator down to the ground floor, and the two RCMP officers shook my hand at the door.

"If you think of any way to help, let us know." McIlroy was overly friendly. Pratt was silent, waiting.

"We will be in touch again," I said, "but the next time I'll call you. I have your number." Then I left the building, my mind in turmoil, and walked for quite some time. It began to rain gently again.

That meeting remained long on my mind. I remembered almost every word. On recollection it had not been that unpleasant. I might have been a little truculent, but then I could afford to be. I had nothing to hide. At times I felt it was I, not the RCMP, who had held the interview.

In the lobby of the Château Laurier I found a secluded corner, took out my notebook and pocket recorder, and documented what had taken place at RCMP headquarters. Then I went to the phone and called Hugo at his apartment in Quebec

City. An operator came on the line and said service at that number had been discontinued. I tried his office at Laval University but there was no reply.

That evening I decided to search out the truth for myself. Had Hugo really betrayed his country? I was not satisfied with what the RCMP had told me and what little the media reported. Nor would I be satisfied with the verdict of any court if he should be tried. Judges and juries are far from infallible. If there had been any treachery I would find out myself. Block by block I would build the story to its conclusion.

Three weeks later I flew to Quebec City. It took me that long to reach Hugo by phone at his office in the economics department at Laval University. While the university was in session he could be found any evening in his apartment. And that was where we met and talked long into the night. It is to Hugo's credit that he answered whatever questions I asked. Much of what he told me was the truth which he could tell to no other. Some of what he said had to be only part of the truth, and I think he realized I understood this. I asked nothing that I knew he could not answer, and he told me more than I expected. But there were many silences when the truth could endanger him.

I wanted to know if Hugo had betrayed his friends. He never answered that question. For it is easier by far to betray a country than a friend.

– CHAPTER TWO –

The
Visit

MARCH 1980

My pilgrimage to the Hambleton homestead was like visiting a house of ghosts. The house on Ruskin was a small, unpretentious brick structure on a residential street behind the Ottawa Civic Hospital. I had spoken to Bessie Hambleton over the phone and by shouting did my best to warn her of my impending visit. A loud alarm bell alerts Bessie to the ringing of the telephone. Over the years she has become almost totally deaf and consequently one is never absolutely sure whether she hears what one says.

When I arrived at the house, I banged loudly on the door. No one answered, but the door was open. In all the years I had known the Hambletons, it had never been locked. I entered in the belief that someone must be at home.

It was a place I had known and visited countless times as a youth. Each room was as familiar as those in my own home, although I had not been there for a long while. When I closed the door that day it was as if everything had been frozen in time, unchanged since my youth. The tarnished Victorian furnishings, the Canadian paintings of the Laurentian hills hanging on the water-stained wall, and the dining room table and chairs were unaltered. Around that same table each evening, daughter and son had once sat, diligently studying French and Spanish under the tutelage of their mother, a stern taskmaster. On the table was a bowl of shrivelled apples, just like the ones I recalled seeing thirty years ago. Books were scattered at random on the living room sofa, and a half-burned log still lay charred on the grate in the fireplace.

Near the entrance to the living room was a worn brown leather armchair and an adjoining side table where Hugo's boyhood shortwave radio had rested. As a young man he had built his own radio sets and listened, absorbed, for hours each day to broadcasts from around the world. The radio had always been his most important possession. Hugo gained a vast store of general knowledge through his radio, much of it irrelevant. But it had whetted his appetite for foreign places.

An intellectual chasm separated Hugo from most of the boys with whom he associated at Lisgar Collegiate Institute in Ottawa. I suppose I was one of his few friends. Hugo and his interesting family attracted me. Bessie had an intellect of grand proportions, and George Hambleton was a well-known press correspondent who had travelled the world. It was all very impressive to a youngster with an inquisitive mind. My mother was dead, and my father commuted regularly between Ottawa and Winnipeg during the years he was in Parliament. I required more intellectual sustenance than my other friends could provide, and in Hugo and his family this need was fulfilled. (Bessie was a good cook, too.)

Almost every evening the Hambleton household was a gathering place for stimulating guests who came from all over the world: Polish and Czechoslovakian diplomats, aesthetic-looking English and American writers from magazines of the left, Canadian diplomats who were sympathetic to the liberal causes of freedom throughout Europe. Often the living room became a babble of foreign tongues. The entire family would be present—Josephine, the blonde daughter, with a face like a blushing china doll; George, the father, a gentle man who listened and seldom spoke. He had a large white moustache, a mane of flowing white hair and quiet blue eyes. He padded silently over the floor like a Persian cat wearing a pair of furry slippers. Without warning he was liable to vanish upstairs to his study to type out his parliamentary press gallery reports. He went quietly about his business, ignored most of the time by his own family. But dominating any gathering would be the overpowering figure of Bessie Hambleton.

Physically and intellectually Bessie was bigger than any other member of the household. She spoke fluent French, Spanish, Italian, German and possessed a deep intellectual grasp of European politics and economics. This emancipated woman fascinated all her guests, including me. In the family, her first love was her son, whom she affectionately referred to as Hugo. Very early, Bessie had planned out her son's life. He would be an academic, a man whose sympathies were liberal and imbued with the great philosophies that had shaken off the chains of the oppressed in Russia and Mexico. Hugo responded to all of his mother's challenges, which were softly spoken but inexorable. Bessie had a will of iron. She had few plans for her daughter Josephine, who was the older of the two children and who seldom questioned her mother's decisions.

Bessie also turned out to be a shrewd investor, and at an early date she wisely bought a magnificent hundred-acre estate in the Gatineau Hills known as McClosky's Farm. It was seven miles up a wild wagon trail from Meach Lake outside Ottawa. Her investments were to be her son's inheritance so that he could carry out her chosen tasks. She had a subtle way with people, and although she was inflexible with her husband and daughter, with Hugo she developed another kind of relationship, an unspoken understanding that her son must be ready to take on responsibilities that represented man's advancement toward the shining goals of a new social order. Bessie was an omnivorous reader, but I do not remember her son reading very much; rather he was a devoted listener and spent most of his spare time tuning into the foreign broadcasts that came over the shortwave.

I learned later that Bessie was a committed parlor Marxist but more interested in ideology than action. The idea was very remote to me, of little consequence to my life or for that matter, I thought, of little consequence to anyone. But in all the years I knew the family I never heard the word "Communist" mentioned once. Nor had I any indication that anyone in the family had the slightest interest in promoting a foreign ideology. Bessie always struck me as a devoted Canadian, a woman who was genuinely proud of Canada. She took pride in all things that put Canada first and I believe she meant what she said. She hated bureaucracy too much, I thought, to ever be a Communist. Frequently she would refer to Russia in her conversations but only in the vaguest terms. "Too bad," she would say, "that such a glorious experiment failed."

As a youth, I was impressed with my friendship with Hugo. If I wanted to spend a few days in dense bush camping out in the Gatineau Hills, he would agree immediately to accompany me. Once in a blinding blizzard we skied the ten miles from Hull, Quebec, to Meach Lake, climbing on skis through the ferocious storm in deep snow, up the long trail to the Hambleton farmhouse on the hilltop.

We were high-school students then, and I remember one incident the following spring which startled me. We sat on a back bench together in the chemistry class at Lisgar Collegiate, sometimes listening to our teacher Louis Meng. We thought we could talk at the back of the class unnoticed, out of earshot of our instructor. Most of the time he silenced us with biting remarks that frequently evoked snickers and laughter from the rest of the students. Hugo had just finished telling me about his remarkable adventures in an uprising in which he and his sister participated during a recent visit to Mexico. He had produced some fascinating pictures of a mob of peasants marching down a main boulevard when we were interrupted.

"Heaps," came the caustic voice of Mr. Meng, "stop talking and listen to what is going on if you want to pass the exam." Then he added in a particularly sarcastic tone, "You'll never be as great a man as your father."

"I don't expect to be, sir," I said humbly.

A wave of laughter erupted from the class, burying the remark, and the chemistry class continued.

A few minutes later when attention was directed elsewhere, Hugo nudged me. He undid the button on his jacket. Beneath his coat was a large pearl-handled six gun, fully loaded, protruding from an ornately carved leather holster.

"I brought this souvenir back from Mexico." Hugo smiled triumphantly. I thought maybe he was going to blast Mr. Meng right out of the room. I was immensely impressed. He had just turned seventeen; I was not quite sixteen.

Some weeks after the incident, an English touring company of Stratford players was performing Shakespeare's *The Merchant of Venice* in an Ottawa theatre. It was a gala event. On the opening night local celebrities and the diplomatic corps of Ottawa were invited. It was a black-tie occasion, and all the Hambletons attended. For some reason the words Hugo said to me the next day at school have been retained in my mind all these years. I asked Hugo how he enjoyed the theatre.

"I was in evening dress," he answered proudly. "The police cleared a path through the crowds for me and my family. You should have seen the attention I received. The people on the street stared at me. We arrived in a chauffeur-driven limousine with the Chilean ambassador. To be important, Leo, to have people pay attention to you, that is what counts in life."

I agreed, but for different reasons.

Now, years later, I stood in the empty living room, these

memories flooding my mind. Surely the house could not be deserted. I noticed for the first time a pot of tea on the kitchen table. Upstairs I heard a faint rustle of skirts.

"Bessie," I shouted, but there was no reply. I climbed the stairs and found her in the study, bent over a chest of drawers. She was wearing a long black skirt that rustled loudly every time she moved. She straightened up when she saw me. Her hair was black with hardly a trace of grey, her eyes flashed with sudden recognition, bright and alert, and when she spoke her voice was surprisingly strong.

With unusual casualness, she said, "Hello Leo, how are your wife and children?" as if the last time we had met was yesterday and not seven years ago.

"Very well," I said loudly.

"I'm sorry. It's such a nuisance. I can hardly hear a word you say, and I refuse to wear one of those contraptions. You'll have to shout and move your lips actively so I can read them. Otherwise it will be hopeless."

I took Bessie's advice and started shouting and mouthing my words carefully.

"You look extremely well," I complimented, meaning every word I said.

"I broke my hip six months ago, but I'm all right now," she said. She led me down the stairs to the kitchen and poured me a cup of tea from the still-warm tea pot.

"Hugo is not here," she said. "You'll find him in Quebec but he should be back on the weekend as usual."

"I saw him in Quebec."

We sat at the kitchen table together. It was like old times again.

"I thought you might be one of those dreadful men from the Mounted Police. They've been here several times and always travel in pairs. You can be sure they had an awful time with me."

I nodded and replied, "I'm sure of that."

She smiled. "I really don't know what they wanted. They searched the house from top to bottom."

"Did they have a search warrant?"

"One of them flashed an official-looking piece of paper before me, but I couldn't find my glasses, so I didn't know what it said. But it didn't make any difference. They searched the house anyway."

"When did this search take place?" I asked.

"A few weeks ago."

"Was anything removed?"

Bessie hesitated thoughtfully for a moment. All her faculties worked. Neither the speech nor the memory of this remarkable old lady was impaired.

"They took away some of my books," she said, "but they returned them a few days ago."

"Is that all?"

She shook her head. "No, they found some old radio equipment that Hugo had discarded long ago and carted that away too. You know Hugo has been fooling around with radios ever since you've known him. Mutt carried the radio off, and Jeff took the books. The comic characters Mutt and Jeff—one was a big fellow, and the other was a small man."

It sounded like McIlroy and Pratt.

"Did they ask many questions?"

"Only about Hugo. My political affiliations. Why years ago did I teach the Russians English? Can you imagine the stupidity?" She was indignant.

"What did you answer?"

"I said I taught the Russians for the money. What other good reason was there? The Russians always paid well and didn't bargain."

If the Mounties had annoyed her, she no doubt had let them know. Bessie feared no one and would take delight in attacking an arm of officialdom.

"They're a tiresome lot," she said. "I don't honestly think the RCMP know what they are doing."

"Were they after any other information?"

She laughed derisively, a strong laugh that had lost very little of its defiance.

"They wanted to know about my life, some of the things we'd done and the people I had known. I told them if they were serious they had better be prepared to stay for several weeks. I told Mutt I'll be ninety-three shortly, and I've done a good deal during my lifetime. What nonsense at my age to bother me with such foolishness. And they were grown men with notebooks, making note of everything I said." She acted incredulous.

"They wanted information on Hugo," I said.

"Then why can't they ask him?"

"They have," I assured her, "on a number of occasions."

She either didn't hear or chose deliberately to ignore me.

"Have you eaten?" Bessie asked considerately.

I thanked her and assured her I had. But she rose to boil some water, since the tea had grown cold. She walked with a slight limp—the result of her broken hip—but otherwise, her posture was erect, her entire bearing that of a woman several decades younger.

"Do you occasionally see Josephine?" I asked.

She sat down again opposite me. "She comes to visit me sometimes with her daughter. They live across the river in Aylmer. Ricardo used to live with me, but I seldom see him nowadays."

Ricardo was her grandson, Hugo's oldest boy from his divorced second wife. For a second or two I thought her voice might have faltered, but if it did, she quickly recovered. I had known Bessie much longer than my own mother, who had died when I was fifteen. Her household had been closer than my own. But now the loneliness of the place, its sadness, the desolation, made me uncomfortable.

"Do you know Lloyd Delameter?" she asked without warning. "He spent time with Hugo when they were both at NATO. He had some kind of school in Holland and settled down in Paris. I often wondered what Hugo saw in him."

I made no comment since I had never met the man. Perhaps she had some personal reason for saying this.

"Those years at NATO, they were important years for Hugo," I ventured.

"Over twenty-five years ago. The world has changed so much since, it's unrecognizable. Can you imagine making such a fuss over a bit of information that anyone could have obtained?"

This comment about NATO struck me as strange, to say the least.

Bessie's eyes grew bright and fiery. "I always taught my son to be an internationalist, that the barriers between nations should be broken down. There is only one world," she said, "only one international world. Fighting over boundaries, hiding information from each other—all that is obsolete. It makes no sense any more to anyone." Her lips trembled slightly, and her eyes clouded over. "But what difference can it all make at ninety-two? It's such a bore being ninety-two. Everyone treats you like a dithering idiot. You don't, Leo, do you?"

"Of course I don't. And I never will."

We went into the living room, she leading the way with her slight limp. We sat on the sofa together.

"Sit close to me," she said. "I can understand almost everything you say that way. Hugo is not a spy. All the publicity in the papers makes no difference to me, but it makes a difference to his children. They don't deserve to suffer."

"They don't," I agreed.

"I hope now that the press is finished with the story and he will continue to teach in peace and the whole business will be behind him," Bessie said, "providing Hugo doesn't do anything foolish. As long as that doesn't happen, then everything will be all right."

I had no idea then what Bessie had in mind. Was Hugo planning some improvident adventure that he should not undertake? Perhaps Bessie thought he had confided in me more than he had. Or maybe, at last, Bessie was losing the gallant struggle against old age, which would have the final and decisive word.

"Hugo is no Philby. He has done no harm to anyone."

I did not contradict her.

"You are an old friend of my son. One of his few. You are not a person to desert a friend, are you?"

Bessie was too proud a person to plead. But if she would humble herself for anyone, it would be for her son, whom she cherished above all else, whose ambitions she had matched with her own. I had never lied to her before; I did not intend to now.

"No," I said, "I do not desert old friends. But sometimes friendships come under an unbearable strain. I don't know all the truth, but I intend to find out."

A look of mild surprise came over her face at my remark. She had heard and grasped every word. Bessie pushed herself unsteadily to her feet, and I rose to assist her, but she refused my offered hand. Instead, she walked proudly the short distance to the stairs and began the slow climb back to her room.

"I have to finish sorting out the linens," she said disinterestedly. "Please forgive me."

It was time to leave. I opened the door and stepped out into the fresh cool air. Outside, the sun was shining on the front lawn and everywhere along the quiet street the world was at peace, at rest, I felt. From the sidewalk I could catch a glimpse of Bessie in the window, bent over the chest of drawers doing the small task she had set for herself. This would be my last visit to Ruskin Avenue. There was no reason to return.

When I left Ruskin Avenue I drove to the Museum of Man at the end of Elgin Street to seek a little solitude. I wanted to try and make sense out of the past. Too many contradictions were present in the Hambleton case. Either I had to accept Hugo as a stranger—cunning, devious and dedicated to the Soviets beyond belief—or as a dupe, a naïve dilettante who had flirted at the edge of excitement and danger without risking his life. The risks he had taken were probably slight social excursions, casual encounters that might have gradually sucked him up into the central vortex of the Russian espionage system. Nevertheless, the main body of important Soviet spies were recruited early in life, at universities and social functions; they were passed on from one generation to another of Russian controllers. The KGB never let go of their man. MI5 in England had been devastated by a network of British spies recruited at Cambridge years ago. Guy Burgess, Donald Maclean, Kim Philby, Anthony Blunt and Michael Straight, who came from a venerated Anglo-American family, were but some of the privileged few who had been misled at a young age into the spuriously romantic world of Soviet communism.

There seemed to be no end to the young Communist platoons of the thirties whose influence and academic background gave them access to the highest government positions on both sides of the Atlantic. Some had disavowed their Communist allegiance publicly and privately. Others could not or did not wish to shake off the commitments of their youth that stuck to them tenaciously for life. Hugo's character was surprisingly similar in temperament and philosophy to all these men. But there was an exception: Hugo's motivations were never defined. He was a master at disguising what he felt about any subject, and had been that way from an early age. If he hid some momentous secret, that meant he had to be on guard continuously. Forever.

Alone in a museum among the contributions of past generations, somehow the present always made more sense, and I could find reasons for the seemingly senseless acts of my fellow man. It was difficult. But here there was refuge. The great wooden masks of the West Coast Indians were like ancient demons glowering at me from within their glass cages, mocking me for my earthly preoccupations.

I was sorry the RCMP had phoned me that Sunday night those many weeks ago. If they had not, perhaps there wouldn't have been a reason to see Hugo again, and he would have quietly passed out of my life. But that was not to be the case.

Incidents that I had never bothered to recall in our association came drifting into my mind. It was this day in Ottawa that Hugo suddenly began to emerge as a new character endowed with qualities I had never before suspected. I knew that in my own way, using my own methods, I would learn the truth about him.

My friend had a compulsion to please. Shy and embarrassed as he might be, he talked freely when confronted with inescapable facts. I would learn he had spoken on a number of occasions to others some months prior to our first meeting. A senior editor of a popular magazine had already interviewed Hugo on several occasions in a room at the Château Frontenac in Quebec. But Hugo's stories to this man had been inventions: he had been deliberately inaccurate for his own reasons. He used the media for purposes that the Soviets and the Western intelligence services call disinformation. I didn't know then that at this he was an expert.

- CHAPTER THREE -

The
Masquerade

*In the masquerade Hugh Hambleton presented a
portrait of himself as he was expected to be: a
professor who inhabited a small, tight academic
world. Sometimes this life touched the secret life
he led; frequently the two lives overlapped,
coalesced and parted again. Finally, one life
devoured the other. When that happened the
masquerade came to an end.*

1939 - 1971

In our last year at Lisgar Collegiate, Hugo and I had conceived
the idea of joining the Free French Ambulance Corps in France.
The year was 1939. I was still under military age, but Hugo had
turned eighteen. I undertook to find four references that the
Ambulance Corps would accept. Two ministers of the Cabinet,
one deputy minister and M.J. Coldwell, the leader of the CCF
party in the House of Commons, vouched for us. Nevertheless,
our applications were politely rejected with friendly letters of
regret that we failed to qualify for lack of experience.

I went on to the university, and when I became of military
age, I joined the army, losing track of my friend until World War
II was over. By chance I led a rather adventurous life in the
paratroopers and with British military intelligence behind
enemy lines. When I returned to civilian life in Ottawa I was
told by Bessie Hambleton that her son had served in the Free
French Army after all and had spent several years with them in
France and North Africa. I didn't know how he had arranged
this, and I didn't ask. He was always very vague about his exact
role with the Free French, but from the little he told me I

gathered that he had missed the great military adventures we sought and had spent most of his time on administrative duties. Nevertheless, Hugo had worked the idea of a romantic French adventure into his life.

After Hugo's return from the French forces I saw him frequently in Ottawa. I had changed as a result of my experiences; like many others I had matured more rapidly than I should have. The war, the death of many comrades, the devastating battle of Arnhem where I had been one of the few survivors, had altered my life at twenty-one and transformed my values. My character had been moulded, and I intended to pursue my objectives, whatever they might be, with great resolve. But I found my friend the same as when we had parted three years before. He had resumed his position in the old chair in the living room beside a more up-to-date shortwave receiver that he had built. He continued to listen to the world broadcasting systems.

Bessie had restarted her program of French and Spanish after dinner around the large dining room table. She had also become, once again, the *grande dame,* hostess to the government officials and friends of the Eastern bloc countries. Diplomats from the new governments of Czechoslovakia, Poland, and Russia and liberals in Canadian government service came to the Hambleton gatherings as they had in the old days. I remember one attractive, statuesque black-haired Polish woman in her early thirties named Maria Kepinski. She frequently came to the Hambleton home. She was a handsome lady with large calves, a firm round bottom and bulging breasts. I recall her well because she dressed the way I expected a true member of one of the proletariat to dress. She wore no make-up and had large, lustrous black eyes. Some people found her attractive.

"I would like to marry her, live in Poland and participate in the new revolutionary era of that land," Hugo said to me one day out of the blue.

I looked at him oddly and smiled. "You don't believe a bloody word of what you just said, do you?"

"No, but I wouldn't mind laying her though," he responded mischievously. And he did many times until she returned to Poland.

Marriage as an institution had little relevance in Hugo's life. He did not believe in it. But if he had to marry in order to live with someone he wanted, he would do so. In 1948 Hugo began courting the daughter of a high-ranking French-Canadian civil servant in the Defence Department, and he married her that same year. The Beaulieus were Catholic, and the Hambletons had been Protestants for many generations, but not practising. Thérèse's family insisted on a large Catholic ceremony in a major Ottawa church. Hugo accommodated his fiancée by converting to Catholicism for the wedding. Thérèse was thin and elegant, attractive with an oval, sensitive face and a graceful body. I heard the wedding was a big affair; Hugo must have loved the pomp and ceremony. But none of his few friends were invited to this lavish event. That included me.

The summer after the marriage I hiked up the old wagon track with the entire Hambleton family to their hilltop retreat in the Gatineau beyond Meach Lake. Bessie in her long black skirt walked up the steep hill with determined strides, showing her excellent physical condition. When we arrived at the summit, I gazed around at the magnificent panorama. The lakes, the woods, the fields of wild flowers that surrounded the white clapboard farmhouse made the scene an idyllic setting. The Hambletons as a family hiked up the trail to the farmhouse on weekends in summer and winter, as long as the trail was passable. It was the perfect hideaway. Hugo enjoyed it particularly because the height and uninterrupted view gave him exceptional radio reception. He kept one of his radio sets in the farmhouse. Wherever he was he never liked to be without one of his receivers.

Hugo had enrolled at Ottawa University in 1947 to finish his B.A. I had opened Canada's first all-Canadian art gallery and within a year had achieved wide publicity, but no money, as a promoter of Canadian paintings. In 1948 another call sounded, and I went to Israel to help the Israelis organize their army. My trip, which I thought was known to no one except members of my family, leaked out, and Hugo wrote to me in Tel Aviv to congratulate me, saying he wished he were there with me.

I returned to Canada in 1950 with an Israeli wife and no prospects of a job and, having no money to go further, settled in Montreal, which was the closest port of entry. I learned from Bessie that Hugo was studying in Mexico. She gave me his address, and we exchanged a few letters, sporadically arranging meetings in Ottawa and Mexico that never materialized. I visited Bessie on a number of occasions at the home on Ruskin and found her ageing gracefully, as I would have expected. I was informed that her son, with her blessing, would pursue a serious academic career in Paris. The estate at Meach Lake with all its glorious wild acres was sold to the government. The old farm later became part of Gatineau National Park, and the beautiful farmhouse was demolished. The idea that I should never again be able to visit the farm saddened me deeply, but I accepted the news with Bessie's reassurance that her son would soon be able to put me up in Spain. The study of the Spanish monarchy was becoming an academic obsession with Hugo—for some reason it fascinated him—and he intended to buy a home on the Costa del Sol, an apartment in Torremolinos and another in the centre of Madrid. Hugo, fluent in Spanish, was thoroughly at home in any Spanish-speaking country. If I could travel to Spain, I was assured, I could use one of the Hambleton homes for a brief holiday.

Property and living conditions in Spain were cheap in the 1950s, and in those days it was a good place to reside. I respected Bessie's shrewd business acumen. She had bought cheaply at Meach Lake and had made a substantial profit and was now reinvesting to ensure that her favourite child would have an annuity for life to do whatever he wanted. Her judgement of the Spanish market later turned out to be extremely accurate; the residences were really fine investments, in time appreciating ten, fifteen, and then thirtyfold. But the investments came to nothing in her son's hands. When Bessie became too old to travel, she could no longer administer them. Her husband George, a hopeless businessman, had little idea of how to supervise an investment, and Josephine knew even less about business than her father and brother. When Hugo finally assumed responsibility for Mariposa—the butterfly—the beautiful little villa in the hills of Mijas, the apartments in Torremolinos and Madrid, he placed them in the hands of an American real estate agent who lived in Malaga. The agent rented the lovely Mijas house to two homosexuals for a ten-year period at a rent so low that the taxes could not be covered, and the apartment suffered a similar fate. Hugo could not stay in any of the dwellings except by giving long advance notice, which he managed to do from time to time.*

---

*Today, the Spanish authorities have taken over the properties until back taxes are paid. I mention Hugo's Spanish investments because the British press made a great fuss over their value and where the money came from. The luxurious villa in Mijas, worth about $250,000, and the apartments, which had about the same value, provided no income.

The money Bessie so cleverly invested which was to become the basis for her son's security was badly mismanaged, but she still had some investments of her own which she husbanded with wisdom and which took care of all her personal needs. These she held on to and didn't offer to anyone. As for Hugo, he never cared much about money as long as he had enough to live on from one day to the next. His employment at NATO and his teaching jobs seemed to generate sufficient funds to look after his responsibilities and his travels. But he had another source of income that no one knew about until much later.

From 1950 to 1961 I lived in Montreal. Hugo lived in Paris, and from time to time he and I communicated, and I kept in touch with Bessie. No matter what occurred anywhere in the world, somehow I knew that the house on Ruskin would always be standing and that strong and noble woman would always be there to welcome me. As she grew older her conversations turned more to Canada, especially the racial conflicts that were tearing at the heart of the nation. Her concern for the country was that of an impassioned patriot, and she was as indignant about bureaucracy, the Liberal government and incompetence as she had always been. I had the feeling she was growing more conservative.

Her husband was dead, the house had grown silent, and she was alone. She behaved as if she had no further use for those stimulating gatherings I remembered. She occupied herself in her study, working constantly, perhaps on a translation for the government or some other self-appointed task of research. (I never did find out what Bessie so conscientiously devoted her time to in that upstairs room.) Her character remained strong, and when I saw Hugo on those rare visits in company with his mother, it was still Bessie who dominated the conversations and whose word was law.

One of my visits to Bessie was in the winter of 1959. She was seventy-one then but looked twenty years younger. We spoke at length that day and had tea together. She said Hugo was completing five successful years at NATO and intended to leave with the highest recommendations.

She could not travel to Europe that year because she was busy, but she had already joined her son on two holidays in Spain. She and Hugo had had long talks together. He always told her everything. They were friends, she said, and Hugo would always respect her opinion.

"He has a great future ahead, you know, Leo. A great future.

He is going to take another doctorate at the London School of Economics. I urged him to leave NATO. Personally, I didn't like the atmosphere."

I had an instinctive feeling she wanted to talk to me about other subjects but thought better of it. I knew Bessie well: like her son, she never confided. If there was a secret it would remain forever closeted only among the Hambletons.

It was only from Bessie that earlier I had learned that Hugo's first marriage had ended. Then toward the end of his stay at NATO in 1960 he returned home unexpectedly with a new wife, Fiorella, the daughter of a well-to-do businessman from Rome. From the beginning they were not compatible. Their life was chaotic, argumentative, and although the marriage lasted for eight years and produced three children, it never really worked. Hugo could not adapt himself to marital responsibilities, nor could any woman become used to his monastic ways, his emotional immaturity, his secretiveness, and his introverted habits. One had to be a lifelong friend to tolerate these qualities and accept them; a wife would find them impossible to live with.

In 1964, I left Montreal alone and sought my future in London. I was thirty-eight years old and had made a million dollars in the real estate business. But I had lost it all and found myself impoverished with four young children to support and a brave but anxious wife. Throughout my life I had written. My first book, *Escape from Arnhem*, had won a Governor General's Award. A few years earlier a play of mine had been performed in London's West End with some success. The undercurrent of my life was my writing and my interest in art, and I had to find a way to translate these interests into a livelihood to support my family. London seemed to be the place. I had many friends there and somehow felt the intellectual and social climate would be more hospitable than in my native land.

I promised my wife that within a few months I would earn enough to send the fare for her and the children to join me. On Belsize Lane in Swiss Cottage I rented a comfortably furnished flat for seven pounds a week and, with a frenzied and desperate energy, began to look for work.

Shortly after I moved into my Belsize flat I had a visitor. Hugo arrived with his eldest son, Ricardo. Hugo had received his doctorate in economics at the London School of Economics and was on his way to one of his properties in Spain. With some difficulty he had made arrangements to live in his apartment in

Torremolinos on one of those unusual occasions when it was actually available, and had come over from Paris to London especially to see me. Meanwhile Hugo and Ricardo moved into the extra bedroom on Belsize Lane. He had bought a French car while in Paris, and his plan was to leave by ferry in a few days from Dover and drive to southern Spain.

That night we decided to celebrate our reunion, and we went to Isow's Restaurant in Soho for dinner.

Over a bottle of wine I asked Hugo why he had left his good job at NATO to go back to school. He said he had felt restricted by the regulations of the organization. Also, he hadn't liked working for John Licence, his superior. I asked him why. His answer was evasive, but he hinted darkly of homosexual advances that had interfered with his work, and would say no more.

Two incidents occurred during my friend's stay in my flat that I found slightly odd. Among his baggage he carried a large shortwave receiver. I didn't consider that unusual, of course, since shortwave receivers and Hugo were inseparable. They were his link with all those foreign countries whose relationships over the shortwave radio bands represented something important and personal to him. I could understand that. I went to bed early that Thursday evening, at about eight o'clock. Hugo's bedroom was next to mine, so I could hear him tuning in to various frequencies. I could hear Russian being spoken, then evidently the frequency suddenly changed because I heard another voice in English. At the time I didn't think too much about the matter, but much later I learned that eight o'clock on a Thursday evening was a special time. It was Moscow calling.

The next morning I awoke before Hugo and his son and used the single bathroom. In need of a razor blade, I opened Hugo's shaving kit, hoping he might have one. There were some extra blades in his kit as well as a small writing pad. I had never seen one quite like this before: the first page was made of thick, soft paper and below were other sheets like any other pad. Next to it was a yellow notebook. The idea of keeping a writing pad and notebook in a shaving kit was so bizarre that my curiosity prompted me to leaf through the notebook's pages quickly. It contained street names, intersections of corners in Vienna, and several métro stops in Paris. Probably private business, I conjectured, where Hugo in his customary fastidious style had found something interesting he wished to record. Then I closed the shaving kit. It was really none of my business.

That morning at breakfast Hugo revealed that he would be

accepting a teaching post in the economics department at Laval University in Quebec City. He would be one of the few Anglo-Saxons on the staff, and I could see that the idea appealed to him. He was on his way toward achieving all his academic ambitions. According to Hugo, his only problems in life were in his marriage. Nothing on the surface ruffled him, and he attributed his personal difficulties with his wife to her hot Italian blood. The unemotional manner with which Hugo could ignore her explosive outbursts could only be admired, but maybe he provoked them. I never found out. The next day Hugo left my flat with his son, and I did not see him again for quite a few years. He left me with a sudden, unexplainable insight that something in him had altered drastically.

In 1971, I returned briefly to Canada, and I called Bessie. Her son was on leave of absence from Laval, employed by the Canadian International Development Agency program in Peru. Since he spoke fluent Spanish and his specialized field had become economic development of the Latin American countries, Peru was a perfect place for Hugo, but I wondered whether he could judiciously recommend where to place Canadian funds when he had so much trouble with his own small investments. I imagined he travelled regularly from his headquarters in Lima into the countryside and the mountain villages, but as it turned out, he lived in a much more comfortable manner.

1973 - 1979

My fortune, after several years in England, had taken a decided turn for the better. I had successfully published several books that had received critical acclaim, another one of my plays had been produced, and a motion picture script had been sold. I had made some money. My knowledge of the art world had also paid substantial dividends. In England at that period it was still possible to uncover important rare works of art, and I had been lucky. I prospered. My children were growing up, and my wife, transplanted for the second time in her life to foreign soil, was beginning at last to enjoy the country and the people.

In 1973 while I was in America, Hugo invited me to visit him in Haiti. His Peruvian assignment had been so successful that the Canadian government had put him in charge of a CIDA program in that country, as well. "Baby Doc" Duvalier reigned as dictator, dispensing his own personal form of crude, rough justice and patronage from his run-down palace in the centre of Port-au-Prince. Hugo dwelt in the nearby hills in a beautiful white stone villa with his second son, George William, a quiet boy whom Hugo looked after with a rare display of paternal affection. The island was a place of impenetrable poverty where voodoo and illiteracy existed side by side with the brutal secret police known as the Ton Ton Macoute. Hugo showed me around most of the island in his car, saying very little about the poverty that surrounded us and the feudal conditions under which the people lived in their thatched huts by the roadside.

One afternoon we went to an out-of-the-way beach where we could safely swim. We hired two islanders in a leaky home-made boat to row us a few hundred feet off shore. They didn't seem to be in much of a hurry to return to the beach. Instead, they threw out a fishing line and sank back into the boat where they decided to take a nap in the sun. All the while Hugo was looking nervously at the shore about two hundred feet away. I presumed he was impatient to get back, being anxious about his son who waited for us. But that did not turn out to be the case.

The hot sun shining brilliantly in the early afternoon was broiling us in our bathing suits. Speaking in their *patois* French, Hugo urged the Haitians to take us back. But they were disinterested.

"They're fishing for their evening meal," he said. "They can sit around all day waiting for fish to bite. You can't hurry them."

"There's only one answer," I said. And I dived overboard, followed by Hugo.

We swam through the few hundred feet of calm sea to shore, and saw a man wearing a tropical cotton suit waiting in a small clearing shaded by tall palm trees. He greeted Hugo as though he had been expecting him. Hugo did not introduce me, but explained that the man was a motion picture producer making a film on Haiti. He excused himself, and left me on the beach. I didn't attach much importance to the meeting, but the man had the kind of prominent facial features one wouldn't quickly forget.

He was a heavy-set middle-aged individual and, dressed as he was, obviously hadn't come to the beach to swim. He had straight black hair, slightly receding at the forehead, and bushy black eyebrows. High cheekbones gave his facial structure a Slavic look. The man's eyes were hidden behind dark glasses. There was a power and an arrogance in the features.

After a few more interesting days exploring an early archeological find that dated back to the sixteenth-century Spanish conquistadores, I took a plane to Miami and from there caught a direct flight to London. I left Haiti with a good feeling about my friend. He was prospering and was not only a successful academic but was now one of Canada's authorities on the underdeveloped nations of the Americas. I predicted a distinguished career for him to my wife when I arrived home in London. But Tamar was less optimistic. She was not overly fond of Hugo, but she had not known him as long as I had. She worked in the field of marital relations and always considered him a classic example of arrested emotional development. She had engaged him in conversation a few times and thought she could make a number of shrewd observations about his character. Tamar claimed he had never really entered adulthood and still wrestled with the unresolved fantasies of adolescence.

I encountered Hugo again sooner than I anticipated. In the early winter of 1974, he wrote that I could soon expect him in London in company with a friend. In late December I received a call. Hugo had arrived and was staying at a second-rate tourist hotel off the Bayswater Road. He said he had a little business to attend to in the British Museum but could come to see me at my home the next day for tea. After a week in the city he intended to go to Paris, then Torremolinos, and later to Vienna. Austria, as I recall, was to be his final destination before returning to Miami and Port-au-Prince where he had left his young son in the care of friends. His tour of duty for the International Development Agency in Haiti had come to an end.

In a few days it would be New Year's Eve. We had been invited to a party, and my wife graciously suggested that perhaps Hugo would like to join us with his friend, whoever that might be. He was somewhat reluctant to accept this invitation but he did come to the house to visit us for tea as planned. My children were all present, anxious to meet my interesting friend of the academic world. They were especially interested in people I had known in my own youth, curious about my history, which they tended to identify with their own.

Hugo surprised us all when he arrived: his companion was a young, black Haitian woman named Maria Fleuries, twenty-two years old. He shocked me perhaps more than the rest of the family who took his visit calmly and went out of their way to make the young woman feel at home. She spoke only in the French *patois* of the Haitians, which is difficult for any French-speaking individual anywhere but in Haiti to understand. She was attractive, very shy, but hardly uttered a word the entire afternoon in spite of everyone's best efforts to put her at ease. My sixteen-year-old daughter had more in common with Maria than my wife or I did. Personally I was embarrassed, but my friend was unconcerned. After a few minutes, I asked him who this girl was.

"She's a hostage," he said seriously.

"What?" I didn't think I had heard correctly.

"Hostage," he repeated. "I left George William with her parents, who are relatives of the Duvaliers in Haiti, and one of the few important families on the Island. He is safe as long as I have her with me. Do you follow?"

I was somewhat astounded at the reasoning. What had he done that would require this peculiar exchange? I refused to take his explanation seriously. Perhaps this was the best excuse he could make up at the time.

"Her family think I intend to marry her," Hugo added without a change of expression. This was hardly the time or place to comment. Either Hugo thought I was very gullible or there was another reason, since every move Hugo made was calculated. It would all make sense only when the masquerade was over.

My wife eyed me nervously. She was impatient for the tea party to end. I recalled having seen the girl once before, briefly in Haiti. She lived in the exclusive compound near Hugo's villa. At least that part of the story was true. But I wondered how she had been allowed to travel to Europe so readily. The few ruling families of Haiti are devout Catholics who guard their daughters' morals with the rigidity of religious zealots.

"No problem with the family?" I asked.

"None," Hugo laughed as if it were all a great joke.

Thankfully, the tea party ended, and it was time for Hugo to depart. Out of earshot my wife whispered, "Your friend is crazy."

I drove Hugo and Maria to the Bayswater hotel, hidden in a row of similar seedy dwellings frequented by hoards of Africans and European visitors on cheap package tours. A middle-aged white accompanied by his black girlfriend would not be particularly noticed in this neighbourhood.

Reluctantly I took them both out to dinner that evening to an Indian restaurant not far from the hotel. I wished to reciprocate Hugo's generous hospitality in Haiti, but it was more a duty than a pleasure.

Several times that week Hugo phoned. He seemed nervous, but he never told me what bothered him, and I didn't expect him to do so. His personal life, always in chaos, now appeared to be scrambled into an irretrievable mess.

My friend joined my wife and me at a New Year's Eve party at the end of that week, wisely leaving Maria Fleuries at the hotel. He said she felt ill at ease in company. I could believe that. In a few days they would be leaving for Paris, then on to Spain. (A story Hugo circulated later was that Maria entered a Spanish convent to become a nun. All his women were in one way or another conveniently disposed of through elaborately contrived stories.)

The hostess at the New Year's party lived in a quaint old house in Chelsea off the Fulham Road. Because she was born in Russia, she spoke the language, and her English still had a noticeable Russian accent. She discoursed freely about the Bolsheviks of her youth, and the more she drank the more she recalled about the Revolution and her childhood in Moscow, recollecting every street by name. She was delighted to have a Laval University professor at the gathering, and since she also spoke fluent French she did her best to engage Hugo in conversation in that language. But Hugo treated the charming hostess as if she were an intelligence officer interrogating him. His answers about Laval, his work, the Parti Québécois were couched in equivocal, ambiguous terms. He was decidedly ill at ease at a party where one would have expected him to be more forthright and relaxed. He didn't even touch a drop of champagne all night. When the time arrived to leave, Hugo acted as if he was deeply relieved at the opportunity to escape.

In the early winter of 1977 my work took me to Quebec City. I was working on a new book, a novel called *The Quebec Plot*, and I could think of no one more capable of helping me with my research than Hugo. The book was about a fictitious uprising in Quebec organized by a Canadian revolutionary group, and I needed information about the city, as well as political analyses as to what was happening that year and what might possibly occur. I required factual material about army units stationed in the province, about various types of commands and their locations. As a Canadian who had served in several wars and had been present in a number of uprisings I was conscious of the possibility that para-military groups could be in training in northern Quebec or that the Russians could find Quebec a fertile breeding ground for subversion.

I was sure Hugo could answer some of my questions. I wanted accuracy and realism in the story, and I knew Hugo always had a keen interest in military matters. In fact, he collected many different military journals as a hobby. I didn't question why he had such a voluminous supply of material very conveniently suited to my purpose. Piled on the floor of his St. Foy apartment were stacks of pamphlets, some issued by the Department of Defence, others by various military institutes around the world. The answers to all my inquiries were easily found in one or more of the dozens of publications he had conveniently collected for his own use.

I was Hugo's guest for several days. During my stay I wanted to discuss the volatile political situation in Quebec in depth, but he scrupulously refused to be drawn into any discussion about the Parti Québécois. I knew Hugo, by training and inclination, to be an internationalist in public. In private, I expected him to be a little more forthright, but he was not. He seemed to react to my questions in the same way as he had reacted to our Russian hostess at the New Year's party in London. I know when a man is on his guard, but I couldn't figure out why he should be. I eventually attributed his reticence to the sensitivity of his position as an Anglo-Saxon teaching in a French university.

Late one evening we decided to go for a drive so that Hugo could help identify some of the locations I wanted to use in my book. We went up to Montmorency Falls, across on the ferry to Lévis, and drove back to the Old City. By dinnertime he was more relaxed. We dined out sumptuously that night and discussed my project. I pressed him for any small pieces of information that related to the possible subversion of the government of Quebec by a foreign power. Cuba, I suggested, could be used by the Russians for that purpose. He knew a great deal about Cuba and its intelligence service and eventually supplied considerable detail. When I pressed him on possible Russian aims in Quebec, however, he was much less forthcoming, deflecting the conversation to speak freely of the penetration of the French intelligence service into the province. He didn't like the French. But he knew a surprising amount about them.

Military exploits and daring deeds held a singular excitement for Hugo. To my knowledge he had never participated in dangerous exploits himself, but he admired the courageous wartime exploits of others. His academic curiosity and knowledge about military and intelligence matters I therefore found consistent with the pattern of his life.

With hindsight, I find it odd that in our long and wide-ranging conversation on matters that were of intimate concern to him, he never let slip any hints of his other life, at least none that I could pick up on. He was always an exceptionally private person. Maybe that was the only way he could live, sheltering one life from the other. But to hide a secret life from a friend requires not only discipline but training. Sometimes the best of the trained slip up in a moment of relaxation, but Hugo never did. He didn't normally drink, with the exception of a little wine, and even with a few glasses of wine he tended to remain tight-lipped and controlled. That night was no exception, and neither was my last night in Quebec when I ordered a bottle of claret and, since I am largely a teetotaller, found myself filling up his glass continually until the bottle was empty. Next morning I would be leaving for Montreal and then New York, whence I would return to London. So it was a kind of farewell dinner.

"We are all returning finally to Canada," I said. "It's been a long absence. Fifteen years."

"England has been good to you."

I agreed. "I will be in London for another year, off and on, while my wife moves back."

"I should be over there this summer," Hugo said.

"Alone this time I hope."

He stared at me with a sheepish grin.

"Yes, alone," he said finally.

I told him that my flat in the Barbican should be free, and we arranged a date and place where he would pick up the keys in case I should not be in London.

"I intend to go to the Middle East in June or July. I want to do a little research in Israel and Saudi Arabia on the world oil market."

"Saudi Arabia I can understand for research in the oil market, but Israel?"

"I like Israel. I have some work at the Hebrew University in Jerusalem to finish. After, I hope to travel to Yugoslavia to visit my girlfriend."

At this point I didn't know he had a Yugoslavian girlfriend. He then told me her name was Lili Galeva and showed me a photograph. She had a swarthy complexion, high Slavic cheek-bones, thick lips and dark large eyes. But she was very ill, Hugo told me sadly. He had proposed marriage before he had learned that she was suffering from terminal cancer. She was only twenty-five years old, a tender age, I thought, to have such a terrible disease. He mentioned this distressing news between dessert and coffee, with such amazing nonchalance that I wondered whether he wanted me to take the news seriously.

Then Hugo changed the subject and elaborated on his trip to Vienna after he had last visited me in London. Vienna was one of his favourite European cities, a place he visited frequently. Then we discussed Israel where he had spent a summer working at the Hebrew University in Jerusalem. I was surprised at the extent of his knowledge on the country. Apparently he had made it his business to study the effect of Russian immigrants into Israel.

"Did you ever get to Eastern Europe?" I asked innocently.

He looked at me oddly. "What made you ask that?"

"Just that your mother was always interested in Eastern Europe." I did not consider it unreasonable that some of this interest might have rubbed off on him. It was an innocent question. But he answered tensely.

"I may have an academic interest in that part of the world but I can't say I have much in common with the Eastern bloc ways of life."

I agreed. Hugo would be ill suited to become part of the Communist proletariat. Never in my memory had he ever mentioned the word "communism," nor had he ever shown any signs of any Communist sympathy. The word "socialism" was also missing from his vocabulary, and never once had I heard him speak about any friends or associates from East Europe or Russia. His parents had talked a good deal about socialism when they were active participants in the social and working life of Ottawa. The Hambletons always identified themselves with the CCF party, later the NDP, or the Labour party of Great Britain or the socialist parties of Western Europe. The true social democratic parties I knew from my own upbringing were strongly anti-Communist, although sometimes a good place for Communist sympathies to hide. But Hugo's cold aloofness from any political affiliation, his detachment from all political matters, branded him early in life as someone who had only an academic interest in the subject. In his writings Hugo might have been an acute observer of political events, yet he seldom spoke in depth on any subject—even on Latin America and the Caribbean, his speciality. Occasionally in an expansive mood he would discourse suddenly for five or ten minutes on the plight of peasants in that part of the world, then would fall into silence just as quickly. His personal philosophy was more orientated toward the privileges of the aristocracy, the glamour and association of a patrician life, than with that of the ordinary man.

I surmised Hugo received government grants for his research and busy travel schedule. He had an estranged wife and three children to keep. I never inquired how he could take care of his financial obligations and pay for the frequent voyages throughout Europe and the Middle East. And once or twice I had been curious enough to wonder what Hugo had to do with the man in Haiti and his motion picture business. When I asked Hugo about this, he said he acted as a consultant for a man called Herrmann on the film he intended to make in Haiti. What difference did all this make to me? It should really have made none except that by nature I am an inquisitive person. Hugo's life was complicated, I concluded, and would require the attention of a full-time investigator to unravel. Neither of us knew then that this was actually happening.

Years after our dinner in Quebec City I realized Hugo might have suspected that I came for information on him. In the treacherous game of spying there are no friends and no loyalties. Everyone is a potential enemy. And that is how he must have viewed me.

A small incident should be mentioned that aroused my curiosity briefly that last night in Hugo's apartment in Quebec City after we returned from dinner. The only furniture in his bedroom was a bed and a battered chest of drawers. On the chest stood Hugo's powerful shortwave receiver. The receiver was noticeable because it was the only object of value in the otherwise almost bare room. But the radio itself had not engaged my attention. On top of the set was a small, grey, rectangular steel box with protruding wires connecting it to the radio. I had never seen such an object before. Built into its face was a small glass screen. Hugo noticed my interest. He went into some detail to explain the box was a converter used in foreign countries to convert the voltage of his set. But I didn't know very much about electricity. Three years later, under considerably different conditions, I would see the object again.

I saw my friend only once more—in London in the spring of 1977—before the RCMP security services called me that late Sunday night in Toronto three years later. Hugo had accepted my offer to use my flat in the Barbican. In the event that our journeys to London did not coincide, the keys would be left in the garage office. An attendant was on duty in the underground garage twenty-four hours a day. I had a number of important artifacts and paintings stored in my flat and was worried lest someone unauthorized gain access. But I really had little fear of a break-in. The Barbican complex consisted of several thousand housing units built on a bombed-out site in the east end of London. Once the ancient Romans had constructed their fortifications on that same site. The passageways in the buildings reminded one of the Roman catacombs, while the entrance doors are massive enough for any prison. An infrequent visitor could easily lose his way in the maze of interconnecting passageways, and I provided Hugo with a diagram so that he could find my flat.

Two events occurred during Hugo's visit that I found puzzling and unexplainable at the time. When I arrived in London from Canada that spring I drove from the airport into my underground garage. The spare keys had been picked up. Hugo had already arrived. Sitting on the kitchen counter in the flat was his portable shortwave receiver, but without the metal box. Some books were on the marble table in the living room, and a battered suitcase was in the bedroom. I saw that the bed had been slept in. One suit and some ties were hanging in the closet, and his few remaining pieces of clothing were left in the open suitcase. A few cans of food, milk and a large package of whole-grain health cereal were in the kitchen cupboard. For several nights my stay would overlap Hugo's but that should cause no inconvenience. One of us could sleep on the portable camp bed stored in the bathroom.

Running the full width of the small living room was a balcony that fronted on the new Royal Shakespearean Theatre, which was part of the Barbican complex. The balconies ran continuously down the entire side of the building, each partitioned from the others by a waist-high iron railing, and could only be reached from the hallway where the elevators were located. The only people one ever saw on the balconies were the window cleaners who came monthly and finished their work quickly from the outside. The balconies are too narrow for the tenants to use and are inaccessible to unauthorized persons.

My flat was five removed from the hallway door that gave access to the first balcony of Ben Jonson House, the name given to my building. The balcony picture window is really a large sliding door made of sturdy thermopane glass with a secure lock impossible to open from the outside without breaking the thick double glass. It was a warm day, and one of the first things I did when I arrived in the flat was to slide back the glass doors to allow some air in. The door to my surprise was unlatched. Perhaps Hugo had forgotten to lock it. Although this was unlike him, it was possible. Just to be sure, I checked my artifacts; they were all in place on the shelves.

In the bathroom I placed my toilet articles beside Hugo's small plastic shaving kit, which I recognized. I left a note on the kitchen counter beside the radio, which he couldn't miss when he returned. Then I went about my business.

I had a number of appointments that afternoon, and during the approaching weekend I intended to go to Lymington where I kept my sailboat and prepare it for spring launching. My plan was to sail back to the east coast of America in the early summer. While I dismissed the idea that anything sinister was connected with the open balcony door, throughout the afternoon it made me uneasy. I think now it was probably Hugo's presence that caused the unease, but the elusive feeling of anxiety, which I could not identify, continued to haunt me all afternoon, like some faint fleeting shadow whose gloom I could not dispel.

When I returned to the flat that evening Hugo was there, visibly disturbed.

He had arrived shortly before I did and was frantically searching through his suitcase and shaving kit. He didn't notice my arrival until I greeted him. He had dumped the contents of his shaving kit unceremoniously onto the bathroom counter.

"I'm sorry," he said after a hurried greeting, "I've misplaced a notebook. I've been away doing research all day at the British Museum."

"What does the book look like?" I asked.

"It's a small yellow notebook."

Immediately I recalled having seen such a book in his shaving kit when I lived in Belsize Lane.

"Maybe you left it at the British Museum."

Hugo stared at me hopefully. "Maybe I did." Obviously relieved, he said, "Perhaps you're right." He apologized for his preoccupation and sat down a little less upset.

We settled who would sleep on the folding cot before we decided to go out for dinner. As my guest, I gave him the honour of using the bedroom. I invited him for the weekend to Lymington to work on my boat and he accepted the invitation. At Lymington I would meet my old friend Basil who sailed the Atlantic with me for many years. Basil was a former pilot and wing commander in the RAF whom I learned later was given security clearance during his period of service for atomic research. He had voluntarily retired early from the air force over five years ago and now held an important position in the Civil

Aviation Authority. Basil, as usual, would be available to help prepare my yacht *Heapsea* for the coming season.

Hugo had met Basil on a previous visit to England. I had asked him on that particular trip to speak to Basil before I arrived about repairing the radio on my yacht and changing the ship's batteries, and he had done this for me.

Over dinner I asked Hugo what was in the misplaced notebook that caused him such concern. He informed me that it was his diary of appointments and contacts of people whom he would meet in Europe and the Middle East during the summer. The information was irreplaceable.

As the day had worn on, the slight disorientation from my flight had left me. The matter of the unlocked door had fallen into perspective. It had no importance. But I decided to remind my guest to lock the door whenever he left the flat. When I casually mentioned the unlatched door Hugo reacted as if someone had struck him a blow.

"But I locked the balcony door when I left," he insisted, startled.

"It's easy to make a mistake," I assured him. "You have to push the latch down hard or else it can jump back up again. Nothing to worry about. No harm done."

That evening when we returned to the flat after dinner, Hugo found his yellow notebook. It was inside his suitcase tucked among some unpacked clothes. He had not left it at the British Museum after all. He simply had misplaced it.

Hugo didn't mention the notebook again, but I wasn't altogether certain that he was entirely at ease about the matter.

The next day was Friday, and I happened to be in the vicinity of the British Museum in Great Russell Square. I knew Hugo did his research in one of the small adjoining rooms off the main hall. Whenever I have the chance I visit the museum because it houses some of the finest collections of artifacts and ancient carvings in the world. If one has access to its library and private rooms as an associate, almost any published book is available for research. I couldn't see Hugo anywhere, but the museum is a vast place, and I had not notified him of my intended visit. However, I eventually discovered him in the cafeteria, sitting with his back toward me. He was engaged in an intense discussion with two people on the opposite side of the table. One of the men I had seen somewhere before but I could not place him immediately. The other was a blond stranger. Choosing not to disturb Hugo in such earnest conversation, which I imagined concerned his research, I left and went on my way. Whatever Hugo was discussing absorbed him completely.

From Great Russell Street I walked down toward Leicester Square. The man with Hugo who had suddenly alerted my memory had prominent, unforgettable features. High cheekbones, straight black hair, receding slightly from the forehead, heavy lips, and eyes that were dark and penetrating. I had not seen the eyes before. This recollection hovered on the edge of my consciousness for a while as I struggled to place the face. By the time I reached Leicester Square everything had fallen into place. The man was the same individual who had waited for Hugo on a bench at the beach in Haiti. In Haiti he had worn dark glasses, but the features were unmistakable. It was Herrmann.

I learned later that in 1980 my friend Basil in London received a telephone call from some people who said they worked for the British Foreign Office. They wanted to talk to him without delay. When they arrived, they showed Basil a picture, a bad one, that had been sent by cable from Canada. The men from the Foreign Office asked Basil if he recognized the photograph. Basil didn't because the picture didn't look like anyone he knew. These men also inquired why in a certain yellow notebook belonging to a Professor Hambleton Basil's name appeared in regard to a radio that was to be repaired and some batteries that were to be recharged. Basil hurriedly explained that the radio belonged to my boat, and the batteries were the yacht's batteries. Hugo in his meticulous manner had recorded my instructions. Basil was interrogated one more time and then was left alone. Hugo might have misplaced his notebook for a time, but MI5 knew exactly where it was.

Flat 357, Ben Jonson House in the Barbican, was the last time I met with Hugo before the RCMP raided his St. Foy apartment on the morning of November 4, 1979.

PART TWO

Thirty Years
a Spy

*This was the life Professor Hugh Hambleton
really led and cleverly hid from everyone for
thirty years. This existence was real to him; it was
here he found his true friends, his camaraderie,
his importance as a human being. When he was
finally unmasked, no one was quite sure which
life was the real one, least of all the spy himself.*

- CHAPTER FOUR -

The
Recruit

1949 - 1951

"Vladimir Borodin is a nice young man whom you will meet
this evening," Bessie Hambleton had promised her son. "You'll
like him."

With his wife Thérèse, Hugo had just returned from a year
in Mexico where he had studied at the University of the
Americas. There he had perfected his Spanish and received a
master's degree at the school, and now he planned to seek
employment in Canada, preferably in some government job in
Ottawa. Meanwhile, through his family connections he started
to attend numerous official functions sponsored by foreign
embassies—a lifestyle Hugo found personally pleasing. That
night there would be a gathering, and Bessie wanted her son to
meet the young Russian whom she liked.

Her son was at the beginning of his career. He had taken a
temporary job with the National Film Board, but later there
would be many opportunities to work and study at leisure and
enjoy the income she had established in order to make Hugo a
man of modest but independent means. In good time he would
become an international scholar in the field of economics. Bessie
had taught Hugo in early life that a nation's boundaries were of
no consequence. He would bridge the ideologies that separated
East from West and through his work play an influential role in
society. For people to listen to Hugo he first must be respected
and learned. And to do that he had to diligently apply himself to
his chosen subject.

The young Russian Borodin was a few years older than

Hugo. He had served in the Russian army, and at present he was a cultural attaché at his embassy. He was also a KGB recruiter. This was barely three years after the famous defection of the cipher clerk, Igor Gouzenko, from Ottawa's Russian embassy. For those years the Russians had not been conspicuous at social gatherings. It had taken that long for the KGB to reorganize themselves in Canada after Gouzenko's defection had decimated the organization. The cipher clerk had revealed the names of most of the major Russian spies operating in the West.

It was a lovely spring day in Ottawa in the year 1949 when the Hambletons held their party at their home on Ruskin Avenue. That April afternoon Bessie had finished tending to her tulips in the back garden. The leaves of the tall elm trees were flowering into bud, the front lawn was unburdened at last from the heavy winter snows, and a fresh green carpet of grass gave a touch of lively colour to the old brick house. Soon the whole family would begin their weekly treks up the steep wagon trail to their farm in the Gatineau. Hugo was twenty-six years old, Bessie was fifty-nine.

At the party, Hugo listened to all the interesting conversations without contributing a great deal himself. His mother and sister were always more at ease socially than he and his father. Bessie dominated the gathering with provocative observations about government and foreign policy. First secretaries and their wives from the embassies of Poland, Czechoslovakia, East Germany, Yugoslavia, and a few officials from the Canadian External Affairs Department were present. Once in a while, an ambassador dropped in briefly to pay his respects or a newspaper colleague of the father, George, might come by. The Hambleton parties were multilingual affairs conducted in English, French, Spanish, Italian and German. For some reason none of the Hambletons with their superb linguistic skills had bothered to learn Russian or any of the East European languages.

Vladimir Borodin came as expected, but arrived late. He was the only Russian to accept Bessie's invitation. Another secretary and the ambassador were invited but were unable to attend. Borodin politely offered his apologies for the absence of his colleagues. The Russians were still sensitive about accepting invitations to Canadian homes; they were not overly anxious to be seen in public places and attended only a few private functions, usually in pairs. It was unusual for a lone Russian to show up at a private gathering, but Borodin had decided nevertheless to come, perhaps because the Hambleton home was a place where mixed parties between the East and the West were recognized affairs. The hosts were well respected among diplomatic circles.

In praise of Borodin Bessie had pointed out to her son that the Russian was not like most of his countrymen at the embassy, and those others who came on various trade missions. Borodin was not a boorish, ill-mannered member of the proletariat. Bessie had little time for these types. She enjoyed Borodin's company because his manners, speech and his bearing were aristocratic. Actually, Bessie didn't know much about the Russian, whom she had met two weeks before at a cocktail party in the Chilean embassy where she had been with her husband and daughter.

Borodin was everything Bessie had predicted and perhaps more. He spoke fluent French and English and was courteous in his manner, clearly quite at ease among the guests. He was a slim man with brown hair, friendly blue eyes and delicate hands with the elongated fingers of an artist or musician. His nails were manicured, and his suits were not the ill-fitting heavy brown cloth issue worn by most Russian diplomats. He dressed like someone whose clothes were tailored on Saville Row in London or at Brooks Brothers in New York. He was atypically Russian in appearance and behaviour. He claimed his English was learned in London where his father had headed a Russian trade mission before the war, and he had been tutored in French schools during a two-year sojourn with his family in Paris immediately after World War II. Borodin was intelligent, alert, personable and persuasive. He would be the first KGB connection in Hugo's life and the most crucial. He would also be the most subtle, the most insinuating, and do his job on a willing pupil with the skill of a superb artist. He and Hugo took an immediate liking to each other, and by the end of that evening Borodin insisted they should meet again for lunch during the following week. Hugo, very flattered at the attention, accepted the invitation readily and innocently.

Borodin was older than he looked, thirty-two years of age at that time, but deceptively youthful. In reality, he was a member of the First Chief Directorate of the KGB, which dealt exclusively with foreign operators. Gouzenko's defection had temporarily wrecked, indeed almost dismantled, the GRU, the military arm of the Soviet spy system. However, the KGB was not so devastated, although they still had to act with caution.

The recruitment of spies for field operations in North America had high priority for the KGB. The process of recruitment could last for years, as Hugo would find out. The Soviets were extraordinarily patient. Recruiters like Borodin exercised shrewd judgement, often studying a man for a year or more before approaching him, learning about his background, his friends and enemies, his weaknesses and his strengths. When Borodin was ready to make his approach, he would have learned all there was to know about his proposed recruit. Ideally, Borodin would attempt to find a receptive individual who hopefully would achieve a measure of influence in his own society and perhaps reach a position of trust in government. When that hour arrived, the recruit was expected to fulfill the mission for which the KGB had carefully prepared their man, and they patiently awaited for their reward.

Borodin had travelled to neither London nor Paris as he claimed. His English and French were learned in Moscow at the KGB school for foreign languages. Borodin was a particularly bright and conscientious KGB officer. It is likely that his meeting with Bessie at the Chilean embassy cocktail party had not been haphazard. It had been planned, as had the meeting with her son. The Russian was determined to behave with great discretion and ingratiate himself into Hugo's confidence. He would make no hasty or false moves. The present atmosphere in North America, especially in the United States, regarding Russian spies bordered on the hysterical, and Borodin could not afford to fail. However, the Russian had few fears. He was operating in Canada, not the United States. Once the Gouzenko trial was over, Canadians wanted to forget about their spies. They were not moved to extremes as quickly as the Americans. They didn't like to make a fuss. As a matter of fact, Prime Minister Mackenzie King would have been happy, if he could have, to hand the defector Gouzenko back to the Russians to avoid the inconvenience, had he not been afraid of the adverse effect of international public opinion. Canada was a good place for Borodin. He had a job to do for his homeland, and in Hugo, he sensed he had discovered the right sort of pliable individual he was looking for, with the correct family background, the political naïveté that would make him ripe for exploitation, and a side to his nature that would enable him to idealize cooperation with the Russians as being a romantic adventure.

Yet Hugo puzzled Borodin. He fell into none of the ordinary categories he had been instructed to watch for. His man belonged to no political movement, professed no radical tendencies. He was not a member of any Communist front organizations and expressed no bitterness against Canadian society. Indeed, he held no anger against anyone. He was uncritical of almost all things—a quiet neutralist who shunned controversy of all kinds. If there were deep wells of passion boiling within, they were very well disguised.

However, certain qualities in Hugo appealed to Borodin. The Canadian was tight-lipped and by nature secretive.

There were practically no restrictions on Borodin's movements. Unlike some of his compatriots in the United States, he could move about freely. Ottawa was a pleasant city, and Borodin was extending his contacts and befriending other sympathetic Canadians besides Hugo. Two of Borodin's new acquaintances were young people in Quebec, economists who would be going abroad to study shortly at the London School of Economics. They would later distinguish themselves in Canadian public life. A third individual was a lawyer in Montreal who would become rich and whose partner would be appointed to the Bench. Borodin marvelled at the ease with which he could meet people, travel, and pursue his relationships without hindrance. The casualness of living and the unharried atmosphere of Ottawa impressed him very much. But he was not corrupted by the wealth of Canada; he used the opportunities only to develop one or more reliable agents who would be longtime sources of information.

Two weeks after the Hambleton party Borodin phoned Hugo and suggested they have lunch. They met in the lobby of the Château Laurier and dined below in the Grill Room. The restaurant was always filled with government and embassy officials, and their presence scarcely attracted attention. The popular young Russian diplomat was beginning to make himself known in the diplomatic cocktail circles of Ottawa. His presence at various functions aroused no special interest on the part of the Canadian security service, who in any case didn't have the manpower to keep track of the hundreds of employees from the Russian embassy and their satellites. The RCMP was undermanned and ill equipped to carry out any serious anti-espionage activities.

After lunch, Hugo and Borodin strolled down the pathway alongside the Rideau Canal and sat on one of the benches facing the water and talked. They spoke about everything except what interested Borodin most. It was much too early in their relationship to discuss the topic uppermost in his mind. Borodin displayed an interest in Hugo's future academic ambitions and offered encouragement. Hugo seemed to fulfill the first requirement of a potential spy: he was friendly toward the Soviet

Union, whose massive military power, he told Borodin, he admired in World War II. The Russian sized up his man. His character was certainly unlike his mother's. Mrs. Hambleton was a shrewd, strong personality who held definite opinions on every subject. She was a down-to-earth, practical woman. Her son was more open to suggestion, although he didn't really disclose much about his inner feelings on any subject. But implicit in his conduct was a willingness to please, to cooperate. It wasn't so much what Hugo said that pleased Borodin but rather that what he did not say held promise. When the Russian sounded him out on his political convictions, he found to his astonishment that, unlike his mother, Hugo had none.

When conditions are right, the Russians' courtship of a prospective spy is brief. In this case, Borodin adopted a conciliatory approach. "Canada is small in population but large in area like the Soviet Union and rich in resources. You have vast polar regions in common with my country. The Soviet Union wants a harmonious relationship with the Middle Powers, among which Canada is a leader. Here you and I sit, Hugo, on a warm spring day at peace with the world. Just the two of us. There are no pressures on either of us. I have my job to do, and you will have yours. But how good it would be for the world if our countries could live together peacefully without the threat of any more imperialist wars."

Borodin's misconceived notion that Hugo could be attracted by the idea of a friendly Russo-Canadian cooperation was quickly dispelled. He soon discovered that his new friend had little reverence for Soviet slogans of peace. He could be more easily persuaded to cooperate by arguments of strength. The might of the Soviet military machine and the considerable force of a heartless dictatorship held a strange, irresistible attraction. Hugo questioned Borodin about Soviet military matters but received very few answers that afternoon. Toward the end of their talk the Russian suggested that one day Hugo should consider making a trip to the Soviet Union to see things for himself. The idea received a friendly reception.

They rose from the bench and continued their stroll down the canal. Hugo was silent, seemingly in deep contemplation. The Russian was worried that the young Canadian might have understood at this early stage what he really wanted and grown frightened. Hugo might not have held any deep convictions, but he was highly intelligent. Borodin's suspicious nature took over. Perhaps this was a trap. If he were caught attempting to enlist a Canadian as a Soviet agent, he would be immediately expelled from the country. But he dismissed the idea. The Hambleton family would not be party to such a trick. But Hugo was a much more complex individual than he had originally believed. Borodin would proceed with his customary caution. The next time they met he would advance his cause a little further. The Russian was convinced he would eventually be able to accomplish his appointed task, but it might take years before his man became useful. The KGB were only too willing to invest time and money, a small price to pay for a productive agent. Borodin said good-bye to Hugo, expressing the hope they would see each other again soon.

Borodin's report on Hugo was relayed from the Russian embassy directly to the First Chief Directorate in Moscow. A Hambleton file was opened there very early, before Hugo himself was conscious of his future career.

That same evening before dinner Hugo spoke to his mother. Bessie told her son that she had asked Borodin to join the family on the weekend for a day at their farm in the Gatineau Hills. He offered no objection and said he had lunched with Borodin that afternoon. Bessie expressed no surprise and hoped both young men had found much to discuss at their lunch, but didn't pursue the matter further.

Hugo didn't mind Borodin coming to the farm. Personally he rather liked him, and probably already had a good idea why Borodin had befriended him. The idea that a Russian official had considered him of sufficient importance to give this much attention flattered Hugo. If most of his own countrymen acted with antagonism toward the Russians, Hugo would behave in the opposite fashion. This is the way he would express his individualism and revolt against society. It would be quiet and secretive. No one would ever know the wild thoughts in his mind that evening at dinner when the subject of Borodin was discussed. Even if the other members of his family might have had some sympathy for the Russian cause, it was a romantic notion, on an intellectual and impractical level. The idea of espionage was remote, unmentionable but immensely intriguing. It might frighten some people but not Hugo and would probably not terrify his mother. But Bessie was an eminently practical lady. For her son, her most precious possession, it simply would not be worth the risk. One was liable to get caught. She cherished much higher ambitions. Borodin was simply a good connection. Young, personable, ambitious and liable to rise to prominence in the Soviet hierarchy. Like Hugo, she might have had more than a vague idea of Borodin's intention, but if she did, she preferred not to deal with it. The Hambletons, especially Hugo, had no worthwhile secrets to transmit even if they had been asked to do so.

On the following Saturday afternoon, a lovely day in May 1949, the entire family, except Thérèse, in company with Borodin drove to Meach Lake, parked their car on the lake road and began the strenuous hike up the rocky track to the farm.

Patches of melting snow still lay on the brown, tawny slopes of the hills. The air smelled fresh. The maple trees dripped sweet droplets of sap and overhead the sun warmed the damp earth. The setting was delightful. It was the Canadian forests in the spring.

Because the track often narrowed, they walked Indian file up the sharp incline. Hugo led carrying a rucksack of food for the midday meal. A few steps behind him came Borodin, followed by Josephine and Bessie in her flowing black skirt. Mr. Hambleton quietly brought up the rear. It took about an hour of steady walking to reach the farm on the summit. At the end of the track in a large clearing stood the white two-storey wood house. On either side of the building the ground sloped sharply away. To the west was a lookout from which one had an uninterrupted view over the wooded hills and distant lakes.

Borodin must have been convinced that people did not come to this inaccessible retreat hidden in the hills just because they enjoyed nature and solitude. He did not understand that Bessie, who had bought the property some dozen years earlier, and her family loved the beauty of the Canadian outdoors. There had to be another reason for coming to this isolated spot, but he could find none.

Perhaps he had made a serious mistake in his judgement of Hugo. Why would a young man who had so much want to work against the country that gave it to him? Borodin would refuse to do in Russia what he intended to ask Hugo to do in Canada. But Borodin knew that in rich nations it was exactly the people who had everything they needed who became the most likely sympathizers to his cause. Capitalism carried within it the seeds of its own destruction. Every good Communist knew this. So Borodin didn't bother to question motives. He had a job to perform: to recruit a Canadian who was prepared to betray his country. And he had a sympathetic recruit. It was now up to the KGB officer to enlist his subject in a manner sufficiently subtle so that it would appear innocuous.

After lunch the two young men went for a leisurely stroll together to the edge of the farm clearing. A path led higher up a grassy slope from where they had a superb view of the Gatineau. Below them the world rolled away magnificently into endless folds of green hills and valleys, pure, clear lakes, and tumbling streams. They sat on the warm grass talking on this ideal spring day.

Borodin asked, "Do you know what you want to do next year, Hugo?"

"I will be leaving my job at the National Film Board and go to France to take an advanced degree at the University of Paris."

"Have you thought of applying for a position in External Affairs?"

Hugo might have vaguely entertained the idea but the Foreign Service did not appeal to him. He very much wanted to travel with his wife to Paris. She had never been there. Also Hugo wanted more distinguished academic credentials to attach to his name. The year before he obtained his M.A. in Mexico and now wanted a French doctorate from Paris and later another from the London School of Economics. The KGB officer listened sympathetically, patiently, and praised Hugo's ambition. The notion that Borodin was seriously interested in his long-term future did not cross Hugo's mind. In the relaxed country setting where the silence was broken only by the droning of the black flies, nothing seemed important. But the Russian wished to talk business.

"In my country we are interested to have links with people in Canada who understand the importance of sharing data. You could perform a useful service to both our societies."

The significance of Borodin's remarks registered. In Hugo's future liaison with Borodin the Russian didn't understand that the clandestine nature of the deed was far more important to Hugo than the information he might obtain for the Soviets. Hugo agreed that in principle it was useful for nations to cooperate with one another, but practically there were too many obstacles, too many gaps that separated them in their thinking. Still, Borodin had not offered any definite proposals.

The sun had warmed the earth sufficiently so that the two young men could stretch out on the grass to continue their conversation.

"Between nations, it is important that there are people like ourselves who seek one another's help," Borodin remarked. "We have both fought the Nazi aggressors as soldiers of the Allied Armies during wartime. In peacetime it is our duty to defeat the common enemy of poverty and capitalist oppression."

He waited, but Hugo did not answer. Perhaps, the Russian

thought, he had gone too far, too quickly. Deep in the woods of the Gatineau the discussion must have had the quality of unreality.

Borodin had not served in World War II as a soldier on either the Russian or the Western Front. He had proved his loyalty to his superiors as a trusted servant of the regime since his days as a young organizer of the Komsomol, the Communist youth movement. As a member of the old NKGB in wartime, he had overseen part of the Russian internal security system. Hugo had worked at various desk jobs in the French and Allied intelligence service in Europe and North Africa from 1944 to 1946. But neither man elaborated upon his military achievements.

Hugo had a compulsion to please his friends. He wanted Borodin to like him, to accept him as a person whom he would respect as an equal. Russia was one of the two great powers of the world and to be associated with that country through an official like Borodin pleased him. He didn't seem interested, and never would be, in making any moral judgement of the Soviet regime.

"I don't really know how I could be of help," Hugo replied after a long silence. And he really didn't.

That was the reply Borodin had hoped to hear. If not these exact words, similar ones. The important part of Hugo's answer was that there had been no outright rejection.

Borodin dropped the subject altogether for the time being, pleased that he had already established a good friendship with his man.

It is more than likely that he had the feeling he should first ask Hugo's mother's permission to proceed further. Undoubtedly she was the dominant member of the family but she might have been also the first to disapprove. She would be astute enough to know exactly what Borodin planned for her son. It could destroy Hugo's career. An agent, Borodin knew, was designed to be trapped. Bessie would also be aware how easily Hugo's vanity would allow him to be manipulated. She was very conscious of all her son's weaknesses, and would protect him to the last. And as her daughter would say years after, her mother "would willingly crawl on her knees all the way to the pope if she could save Hugo."

Of all the seeds the KGB planted during the decade of the 1950s, in Canada more than one would sprout. It didn't make any difference which one as long as that agent penetrated deep into the heart of the enemy.

"It is best," said Borodin as they walked back to the house, "that our discussions remain our private business."

"You don't have to worry," Hugo promised. "Whatever you say will go no further. No one will know."

The KGB official was pleased with his afternoon's work. It had been pleasant and successful. And he was positive it held good promise for the KGB.

Borodin met with Hugo in Ottawa on at least three more occasions before he left in 1951. Their meetings were innocent-looking affairs that took place once in a restaurant on Sparks Street, and once in Hugo's home when the family were away. A third time they walked together again along the Rideau Canal from the Château Laurier. This was the year Hugo departed for his studies in Paris. The Russian's relationship with the Canadian had developed successfully. Hugo had agreed that a career in government service might at a later date be useful and he would, in principle, be willing to cooperate with Borodin. The good will evinced by both men was vague, but Borodin hinted that day as they walked slowly alongside the canal that he represented important interests within the Soviet Union who would be very grateful for Hugo's cooperation. The Russians would be willing to take care of any expenses that the Canadian might have furthering his career through his studies. There was no hurry, he insisted. He would continue to keep in touch with Hugo, whom he was sure had the ability to distinguish himself in his chosen academic career. Impressed by the attention and the calculated flattery, Hugo passively accepted the blandishments. In the mind of the KGB agent no doubt existed that his persistence would be rewarded.

In fact it already had been. Without any prompting Hugo had already performed one small service that proved his willingness to cooperate. Hugo's father-in-law held a high position in the Ministry of Defence in Ottawa. Through the innocent and unwitting help of his wife, he managed to secure from his father-in-law's office at least one document describing a secret sonic underwater device. This he showed to Borodin. Decades later this incident would come to light. The information was not of great military value, but the Russian made a big fuss and treated the document as if it were of importance. He praised Hugo and exaggerated the importance of his first venture into the world of international cooperation. Both men treated this incident as a lark, not an adventure in the dark life of espionage. Many years later, during Hugo's interrogation in Canada and England he claimed he notified his uncle J.R. McKenna, the

Ottawa correspondent of the *New York Financial Post*, of Borodin's approach, and said that the uncle had passed the information on to the Mounties. Unfortunately no proof of this could be found anywhere in the RCMP records.

Borodin one day suddenly vanished without warning. He slipped away quietly out of Hugo's life. Before Hugo left for Paris he tried to reach his Russian friend once or twice at the embassy in Ottawa, but was told that the cultural attaché was out of the country. Hugo was convinced his small flirtation with the KGB was over. It had been unsatisfying and incomplete but full of the promise of excitement, and he had no regrets. With the Borodin connection gone, he would be missing some powerful ingredient that added importance and purpose to his daily life. The adventure was not altogether without the distant fear that the enticements that had lured him on might one day be false and sinister. But then in his youth the fears were somehow unreal, of no significance. Hugo imagined a deep camaraderie in his association with Borodin, as he would with all his other KGB officers. To him, it was as if he were being initiated into the secret rites of a great brotherhood whose mighty arms embraced all humanity.

- CHAPTER FIVE -

The
Spy

1952 - 1958

In 1952 Hugo embarked upon his studies in Paris at the
Sorbonne, which would last for three years. He had become
reasonably fluent in French as a youth when he had attended
school in France when his father had been a foreign correspondent. Now as a mature student he enjoyed, with his wife
Thérèse, the carefree academic life. His mother provided the
funds, and he applied himself to his studies most diligently and
successfully. He had a meticulous manner both in and out of
scholastic life. In a neat, childlike handwriting he kept voluminous notes not only of his university subjects but of his political
observations in a particularly turbulent period in France. One
of his few friends was a fellow American student, Lloyd
Delameter, whom Hugo would be closely associated with during
the entire ten years he would study and work in Paris.

He corresponded regularly with his mother and sister and
now and then with me. Never again did he expect to see
Vladimir Borodin. Unbeknownst to Hugo, the KGB man had
moved to Washington and then London, but through the KGB
headquarters in Moscow was kept informed of the Canadian's
progress. Borodin had not forgotten his protégé from Ottawa
who was still his special charge.

Almost four years passed before Borodin reappeared. And
he knew just where to find Hugo. The year was 1955, and Hugo
was completing his studies at the Sorbonne. The "accidental"
meeting was supposed to take place in Paris in March, near a
corner where the Rue des Ecoles meets the Boulevard St. Michel,

close to the Hotel de Cluny. Here at a certain hour in the afternoon, Hugo could be seen most weekdays, frequently in the company of other students and sometimes alone as he came from his class at the Sorbonne. Borodin had to wait until Hugo was by himself, but he was an extraordinarily patient man. On the fourth day of waiting, Borodin observed his quarry on the Rue des Ecoles accompanied by a female friend. He followed the two students unseen toward a métro station and watched both of them descend to the train. Perhaps tomorrow the Canadian would be on his own. But Borodin changed his mind. This method of meeting was too cumbersome. He had a better idea. Perhaps after all these years the meeting with the Canadian should be made to appear purposeful and more formal.

On the following afternoon Borodin in the company of a slightly older man came to visit Hugo at his home in the early evening when he was sure the Canadian would be there. The visit took place in the suburbs of Orsay about eighteen miles south of Paris. Here Hugo and his wife Thérèse lived in a small rented chalet that was part of a large estate belonging to friends of the Hambleton family. It was a secluded, delightful cottage set in beautiful surroundings which offered considerable privacy.

The knock on Hugo's front door that day in March changed his life. Borodin, smiling and pleasant, stood there with a companion whom he introduced only as Paul. Paul was Russian, but unlike Borodin his English was American and accentless. Hugo would never disclose Paul's real name to anyone. This man for twenty-one years would have an influence on him unequalled by any other person except his mother. In many ways Paul would replace the dominance once exerted by Bessie. But on that day in Orsay there was no hint of the role this KGB official would play.

Hugo politely invited his two guests into the house for a drink, forgetting to ask Borodin how he knew his address. But he thought his mother probably gave it to the Russian. However, his whereabouts had been known to the KGB from the time he arrived in Paris with his wife.

The meeting in Orsay was social, and Borodin and his companion discussed Hugo's career. What did he intend to do when he graduated that year? Paul described himself as an official who was part of a Russian trade mission which would be in Paris for at least a year. It was evident at this meeting that Paul was the senior of the two men. No business of any kind was discussed. But it was Paul who invited the Canadian out for lunch the following week. A date was made to meet at one o'clock on the next Thursday at the Luxembourg métro station. From there they would go to a fine restaurant nearby. Hugo accepted. Thérèse, who was always decidedly nervous in the presence of Russians, declined the invitation. (The intervention of the KGB into his life in 1955 would be one of the reasons for his impending separation from his wife, but not the only one.)

The appearance of Borodin and his companion had lifted an unconscious burden of anxiety from Hugo. Frequently he had wondered about those earlier days in Ottawa and speculated whether his fatal fascination with the Soviets had ended when he left Canada. Hugo and Thérèse had enjoyed very much their Parisian sojourn. They had travelled frequently to the south of France and Spain. His house in Mijas and the apartment in Torremolinos were added incentives to holiday in southern Spain. Hugo's intention after he graduated from the Sorbonne was to attend the London School of Economics to obtain his Ph.D, once again developing his Sorbonne thesis on the Spanish economy but concentrating his attention on the sixteenth century. Hugo, always an excellent student, graduated with honours from the Sorbonne. He had been awarded a Leverhume Scholarship in London the following year, but the unexpected arrival of Borodin in the company of an obviously senior official delayed his plans.

The meeting with Paul at the Luxembourg station took place as arranged. From there the two men went to a small but excellent Russian restaurant called "The Troika" near the faculty of law at the University of Paris. Paul acted as if he was well acquainted with the restaurant and as if the environs of the city were familiar to him. His French was fluent, and his behaviour was that of a debonair man-of-the-world.

The discussion at lunch centred largely around Hugo's future plans in which Paul showed a personal, almost fatherly interest. What did he intend to do? Hugo told Paul of his enrollment in the London School of Economics. He had already submitted the subject of his thesis officially titled "The Economic Decline of Spain in the Sixteenth Century." Paul listened politely, attentively. He had a quiet but commanding presence, a firmness and a shrewd judgement. Whoever he was, Hugo would eventually learn that this longtime handler was an amazing man who in the same breath would ask him to undertake the most compromising tasks, then speak about his devotion to his wife and children who lived in Moscow, and how little time he spent with them because of his work. The impression he gave was that he travelled throughout the world keeping appointments with people he had known for a long time who had important business with departments of the Russian government.

When Hugo finished talking, the Russian complimented him. He said he was so impressed with Hugo's plans that he would be willing to contribute money to pay for his education. But for the time being perhaps Hugo should take a rest from his studies. His enrollment at the London School of Economics should be delayed for a year or two. Instead, he should apply for work at the North Atlantic Treaty Organization in Paris. There he could be of real service fulfilling the tasks of mutual cooperation discussed with Borodin those years ago in Ottawa. Hugo accepted the suggestion, anxious to please Paul, who was undoubtedly a man of considerable influence. If Hugo should at any time run short of money, suitable arrangements could be made to supply whatever cash the Canadian needed. Paul was as magnanimous as he was persuasive in his dealings. He acted as if he could command whatever he needed and spoke with an undisputed authority.

With the help of his friend Lloyd Delameter, whom he had met at the Sorbonne and who now worked in the Economic Secretariat of NATO, Hugo applied for a position. He sent off a letter on April 2, 1955, to a Mr. René Sargent, director of the Division of Economic and Financial Affairs, at the International Secretariat of NATO, Paris. The letter read in part:

> It is with great interest that I learn of the role played by your division within NATO, underlined in *NATO: the first five years, 1949-1954* by Lord Ismay. Since I will shortly be finishing my doctorate at the faculty of law in Paris, I am particularly eager to offer my services as an economist to an organization such as NATO which contributes so directly to the defence of the free world. If at the moment there are no openings in your division, I would appreciate the privilege of working under your direction without pay.

This would result in an interview with the man whom he would work under at NATO, John Licence. Hugo saw him in April 1955 and again in July of 1956. These interviews resulted in his employment at normal NATO salary. The Canadian received his security clearance and was hired officially in a letter sent to him on November 14, 1956.

As an employee of the North Atlantic Treaty Organization,

created for the purpose of a collective self-defence of the Allies, Hugo was obliged like all NATO employees to sign an oath pledging his loyalty.

Much later Hugo, with a typical gesture of patrician loyalty, absolved Delameter from any complicity in his activities. He said, "I got to know him as an unsuspecting person taking the same courses as myself in 1953 at the University of Paris."

The KGB was the world's largest and most powerful secret army. Paul had asked Hugo to become part of it to help Russia in the formulation of policy that would shape the affairs of the world. The idea overwhelmed Hugo.

Paul had said: "You cannot exclude my country from information that rightfully belongs to her. We burnt our villages so the Nazi hoards would not have them. We sacrificed ten million Russians in a war to bury fascism forever. The world must not be allowed to forget what we did."

He meant what he said. But these were not the reasons for Hugo's compliance. And Paul had conveniently omitted to mention that Russia only fought after Germany broke the Russo-German Peace Treaty and attacked first. Then, Germany betrayed Russia. Now the KGB wanted Hugo to betray the West. But none of this mattered. The Canadian had no feelings of betrayal, of morality. He rationalized what he intended to do by telling himself that NATO information *should be* made available. His work would deal with harmless economic matters. Beyond that lie that he told himself was the grander attraction of the KGB that lured him on. Its embrace was deeply comforting and always would be. It gave him strength. He didn't stop to dwell on its purposes, which were devoted to the sinister arts of subversion, spying, torture and execution.

Paul gave no address where he could be contacted. Instead he arranged a series of rendezvous two weeks apart at eight o'clock in the evening at five different métro stations in the northern areas of Paris. The stations were all in the eighteenth and nineteenth districts, the working-class suburbs that voted predominantly Communist in the national and civic elections.

Hugo was given a small map of the city where the stations had been circled in blue ink. No dates or times were inserted. The meetings would commence one week from Friday and would continue until all the stations were used. Then the process would be repeated. If for any reason neither of them could keep the appointment, it would be altered to the following week at the same time and would be changed to the next station in the sequence. This was a clever and simple device. The first station was Clichy, and with each meeting the rendezvous moved eastward along the route of Boulevard Rocheouart toward the Danube station on Rue David d'Angers.

Two intelligence services believed that the real name of the Paul Hugo met in 1955 was Pavel Pavlovich Lukyanov, but no one was sure. He held the rank of colonel in the First Chief Directorate of the KGB. Paul was a few years older than Borodin, probably in his late thirties or early forties when he first saw Hugo. He was much less delicate in appearance than Borodin and unlike his colleague had black hair and more distinctly Slavic features with a wide forehead and thick eyebrows. Decidedly of a more authoritative nature, Paul had none of the superficially gracious characteristics of his Russian subordinate. But if he had to, Paul could be most charming. Hugo responded to Paul's commanding manner from the beginning, as if he were already a trusted servant in the KGB army. An experienced and if need be ruthless spymaster, Paul knew from early in their relationship the weaknesses and strengths of the Canadian. He had carefully studied the entire background of the man who would be under his control and whose life he would manipulate. The Russian knew exactly what he wanted and how to exploit his agent.

One cold evening in February 1957 at the appointed hour of 8 p.m. Paul joined Hugo at the entrance to the Juares métro station. They walked swiftly along the Avenue Jaures in the direction of the Bassin de la Villette until they came to a small café populated by a working-class clientele. This would be one of the rare occasions when they failed to dine at a high class restaurant. Here Paul instructed Hugo to conduct himself modestly and inconspicuously at his new place of employment. He was in no great rush for information. No one could risk compromise. For the first month he would request only an oral summary of documents of low classification whose choice he would leave to Hugo. Paul gave the impression that he knew already a great deal about the operation and organization of NATO. He knew there were four categories of documents; the most important was called cosmic. Below cosmic were the classifications secret, confidential and restricted. Under no condition must Hugo arouse anyone's suspicion by immediately requesting to examine the cosmic documents. Hugo was to read at his leisure the lowest classifications, which would not attract undue attention. No notes of any kind were to be taken for the time being and no files signed out in his name—yet. Paul's instructions were to memorize the contents of a single "restricted" document and on the next meeting give an oral summary. Hugo accepted Paul's authority without question. The Russian would make the ultimate decision himself about the type of file to examine. Hugo didn't enquire how Paul knew so much about NATO.

"In the not too distant future," Paul added, as they left the café, "I will give you further important instructions."

At that meeting no more was said to Hugo of substance. But the firm voice of the KGB was established. If Hugo at any time in his relationship with the KGB had the opportunity to turn back, this had to be an important moment of decision. A choice was still open to him.

Hugo would have access to a major fund of secret information concerning military and economic assessments of member nations, military equipment and resources of the armies of NATO countries, contingency plans for possible economic emergencies that could face Western Europe. This was only a small part of the intelligence available in the NATO documents. Hugo had not yet read a cosmic file, but he could imagine the wealth of material that would be of value to the Russians. So far he had done nothing to seriously compromise himself. The meetings had been harmless but exhilarating. But Paul, Hugo felt, was a man who could be dangerous. He could expose him to his superiors at NATO—and this would cost him his job and blight his career at its very inception. He would be followed by suspicion for the rest of his life. However, Hugo's fear of the KGB was tempered with a desire to be a part of that organization. Furthermore, he liked Paul and would at a future date actually protect him. But the KGB had waited almost a decade for their protégé to reach a position where he could serve them. They would not have let him go willingly now, no matter what Hugo might have chosen to do.

Hugo claimed that for a few days he toyed faintly with the idea of speaking to his superior, John Licence, about the Russian, but he didn't think Licence would understand; nor did he wish so early in his appointment to create an incident. But he really was not serious about exposing the Russian to his superior. Licence was an effeminate, aesthetic character, a quiet man who abhorred publicity and attention. The powerful character of Paul triumphed easily.

Hugo found Licence's personality unattractive, but the man

didn't bother his subordinate with instructions. Also, a false rumour prevailed that because Licence had once known the spy Guy Burgess he could have had a liaison with the Russians. This had the effect of being a further deterrent for Hugo, if indeed he needed one to begin with.

Paul knew that sooner or later Hugo's need to please and serve the KGB would exceed their demands. And it did. The Canadian would provide the initiative without prompting, genuinely believing the KGB would always shield him from danger.

One Friday in March Hugo arrived at Clichy métro station to keep his appointment with Paul. From Clichy the men continued on by métro to the Palais de Chaillot. There, off one of the squares, Paul conducted the Canadian to a fine restaurant. The Russian was familiar with dozens of the best eating houses in Paris. In the five years Hugo was at NATO Paul seldom went back twice to the same restaurant. He was a gourmet, and he always had lots of cash on hand to entertain. On more than one occasion as they dined Paul would pass an envelope containing $500 or $1,000 in hundred-dollar bills, which he insisted Hugo use for travelling expenses. Although money was never an important issue, Hugo never refused the payments.

In the Palais de Chaillot restaurant Hugo summarized in his concise manner the contents of a single classified document dealing with the coal production in Belgium and France for the year 1956. These were two of the countries that came under his jurisdiction. None of the information was of exceptional value. Nevertheless Paul was impressed both by the Canadian's memory and by his thoroughness. The pleasure the Russian evinced gratified Hugo more than he cared to admit. These clandestine trysts at the métro stations, the preparation leading up to them and the ritual that surrounded them became the focus of his life while he worked at NATO. All else was of secondary importance.

The two men continued on a regular basis to see one another throughout the year, and at each meeting the Canadian divulged a little more of NATO's secrets in both written and oral reports.

At La Chapelle near the Gare du Nord in April Paul arrived carrying a plastic shopping bag. Inside was a large Leica camera manufactured in East Germany, and two dozen rolls of 35-millimetre film, each with 36 exposures. Enough film for 864 photos. Henceforth, Hugo was to concentrate on more highly classified files. They were to be signed out at the end of the day, photographed at home, and returned to NATO early next morning to the registry. No other camera or film should be used.

Hugo faithfully carried out his assignments, and by the end of April 1957 had photographed over seventy documents in a small closet on the upper floor of his house in Orsay which he fitted out with special lighting equipment. His wife Thérèse had returned to her parents in Canada the year before, and aside from a housekeeper, Hugo was alone. The exposed roll of film would always be handed over to Paul or a second individual whose name Hugo never learned at one of the regular métro meeting places. If Paul did not show up, another KGB man would identify himself saying simply, "Paul has sent me for the newspaper." Wrapped in newspaper would be the roll of film which Hugo would hand over without a word and immediately vanish again into the crowds.

In May of that same year in a small, exclusive restaurant near Pigalle Paul was in an amiable mood. He told Hugo that he would be out of the country for a month but would return in the summer. Under no conditions, however, was Hugo to miss the next meeting. He should not fail to be in Paris in June and must curtail any other engagements for that period. Then expansively but benevolently Paul expressed his considerable pleasure at Hugo's favourable progress. He confided that he had been asked to communicate the personal compliments of his superior, who held a high rank in the KGB. Paul beamed happily. Hugo's achievements reflected well upon himself. And then the Soviet ordered a bottle of champagne, and the two men indulged in a splendid meal. During the course of the dinner Paul hinted that officials in the Kremlin were reading the reports that Hugo so diligently photographed. Henceforth, he said, the documents taken home should be upgraded to the top-priority classification.

"Cosmic?" Hugo whispered.

"Only rarely," Paul cautioned, "their regular removal might arouse too much suspicion." But he did not dissuade Hugo with any real conviction.

Hugo didn't enquire where the Russian would be going on his journey, but presumed he would be returning home. Actually, Paul was leaving Paris in a hurry because a KGB major, Anatoli Golytsin, whose code name was Kago, had defected in Helsinki and given the American Central Intelligence Agency the names of all the major KGB agents in France, including some Frenchmen and several foreign agents the Soviets had recruited. Paul, however, would not be suspected, nor would Hugo. The Canadian continued his employment at NATO unaware of the tremors that reverberated throughout the spy networks of Europe.

As they left the restaurant after dinner, Paul discreetly handed Hugo an envelope, which the Canadian slipped quickly into his coat pocket. Then the Russian departed hurriedly without a further word. When Hugo opened the envelope at home, he found a thousand U.S. dollars in hundred-dollar bills.

Life at NATO was not lonely. Hugo and his friend Delameter saw a good deal of one another and enjoyed the night life of Paris. Occasionally John Licence would invite Hugo out for dinner with several other associates like Jean Coté, who was from Quebec and shared the same room in the Secretariat at Porte Dauphine. Frequently the documents Hugo took home were signed out by Coté, whose name appeared on the NATO control sheet instead of Hugo's. The control sheet would read "J.C. pour H.H." Coté would never be aware that these documents were removed secretly from the NATO complex, photographed and taken back the next morning. In later years at Hugo's trial at the Old Bailey, the prosecutor would state that this method of signing out reports was a deliberate ruse designed to divert attention from Hambleton and cast suspicion on the innocent Coté.

The meetings with Paul resumed when he returned to France in the summer of 1958. Documents photographed and given to the Russians in one year included embassy appraisals of political parties in the Western democracies, parts of cosmic files denoted by their special top-security red bands, and a highest-priority M70 report of military force objectives projected for the year 1970. In late 1958 Hugo gave Paul one other item that seriously endangered the lives of intelligence agents in Estonia and Lithuania. This photographed document revealed the names of agents in those Baltic nations who provided NATO with intelligence reports. Between 1957 and 1958 Hugo turned over 750 photographs of single pages of NATO documents to Paul and maintained this average for four years, quite a windfall for the KGB.*

---

* NATO security was so poor that within forty-eight hours the KGB could have in Moscow whatever report it wanted. Although Hugo did not know it, a copy of the registry book referring to files by their code numbers was already in the possession of the KGB. Golytsin proved how familiar he was with NATO documents. The CIA gave him a dozen NATO documents to examine for the period 1958 to 1959. Some of the documents were deliberate fakes and others were genuine. Golytsin immediately picked out the genuine ones.

As the Canadian became more familiar with the operations of NATO he also became more confident, more certain that he could obtain almost anything he wanted when he wanted. Until early in the year 1958 Hugo largely exercised his own discretion regarding the files he removed and took home. It was not until the end of that year that Paul issued new instructions. Henceforth the KGB would ask for a document by referring to its file numbers in the NATO registry.

The implication was clear. Although Paul never said so, it seemed obvious to Hugo that the KGB had someone working directly in the registry at NATO. (In 1960 this man would be caught. The spy was a clerk named Jacques Paques who would be sentenced to life imprisonment by a French court in 1961.) Now Paul could request at will whatever document he wanted, and Hugo would have to ask for it from the registry. This meant that the KGB had increasing supervision over the Canadian's role. For the first time some of the glamour may have begun to wear thin as the danger increased. The vice he was caught in could be tightened any time Paul pleased.

1959 - 1960

The summer of 1959 was a busy season. Hugo had spent several weeks travelling in Spain, Belgium and Italy. In Paris he had met Fiorella Marcia, daughter of a Roman businessman who operated a large, prosperous trucking firm, and now was courting her in Rome. They were making arrangements for their wedding later that same year. While in Rome Hugo deposited several classified NATO documents at the Soviet embassy.

The initial fear Hugo felt at the presence of another Soviet agent employed by NATO who could watch his own movements gradually subsided. He knew it was no one who worked near him and might never affect him. The identity of one Soviet agent was always hermetically sealed off from another.

Nothing at NATO really changed. During the day Hugo carried out his duties satisfactorily, and at night completed his assignments for the KGB. He had long since passed the point of no return. But he did visualize a more dramatic role for himself in the KGB hierarchy than as a mere pilferer and photographer. His KGB function was becoming routine, sometimes boring, unimaginative, and he wanted a change. If he was careful—and he was that by nature—there was little chance of being caught.

The bond of loyalty so necessary between a controller and

agent was being constantly tested and strengthened. Paul possessed the perfect temperament to govern the Canadian. He was forceful and wasted few words. He could be a comrade and a father by turns. His requests were more like orders but he was also generous and friendly. His brusqueness was not obnoxious. The Russian represented the ideal figure of authority to direct the destiny of his protégé.

In June 1959 on a Sunday afternoon Paul drove Hugo in the company of an unidentified third man from the pick-up in central Paris toward the woods of Fontainbleau.

Ostensibly the men on this warm day were on their way to the woods for a pleasant picnic lunch packed in a suitcase in the trunk of the Russian's car. Paul's third companion on this odd journey was a taciturn, balding stranger who spoke only Russian and who would be the last person Hugo would choose to accompany him for an enjoyable country outing. The stranger was not dressed for the occasion. He wore a heavy dark suit, shirt and tie and sweated profusely. He had the thick hands and dirty fingernails of a mechanic, and it was obvious he had come to perform some particular function that had nothing to do with a picnic in the woods. Hugo did not ask questions. He would wait until the Russians were ready to explain what they wanted from him.

Paul parked the car on an unfrequented road in the forest and removed the suitcase. Inside was a powerful radio receiver, which was to become part of the Canadian's new spy paraphernalia. The stranger's job was to instruct Hugo in the use of the equipment. The radio represented the latest in Russian technology and had one frequency which, when properly timed, communicated directly with Moscow. Hugo examined the equipment with a clinical interest. He had built many powerful receivers himself, and those he bought he always improved upon.

Hugo was fascinated with this new toy. Along with the receiver came a code book, one-time invisible writing pads and several small yellow notebooks that were the standard KGB issue. This gathering in the forest became a turning point in Hugo's advancement as a KGB agent. As he later said, "The idea of being able to tune in to a given frequency in Moscow, thousands of miles away, and knowing the message was beamed just at me was very exciting."

The stranger explained to Paul in rapid Russian how the set worked, and Paul in turn translated. The instructions were given quickly, and Hugo had no difficulty understanding them. Each Thursday evening at eight, Paris time, he would tune in to the proper frequency to listen for a coded message from Moscow. Each message would be repeated once. If there was no transmission on a given evening, that would simply mean there were no instructions to follow. The weekly transmissions would continue for a period lasting approximately five months. Now NATO documents and film drops at the métro stations and other locations could be requested or cancelled by radio; thus the métro meetings were no longer necessary.

There was also a single code word to be used if Hugo was in grave danger. KGB headquarters in Moscow would warn him by radio. The receiver was an indication of the growing importance with which Hugo was regarded by the KGB.

On no condition must the radio fall into other hands. The mechanic showed Hugo how, by shorting two wires, the entire electrical circuits of the radio could be burned out.

The translation of the code was somewhat complex. Instructions would be transmitted in the form of various sounds to be transferred onto a tape recorder which was part of the equipment. When magnetized carbon passed over the tape, the sound changed into the dots and dashes of morse code, which could be easily read with the assistance of a morse code handbook. The system was cumbersome but safe and worked effectively. From his own knowledge of radios Hugo could easily judge that Soviet technology was still lagging behind the West. But he didn't criticize. The radio gave him mobility. Henceforth he was no longer chained to his Parisian rendezvous.

"There may be periods when you will be on your own," Paul warned. "I will be travelling a good deal during the next year, and I decided therefore that you should carry on in a more independent fashion."

Shortly thereafter the three men returned to Paris, and Hugo took possession of the suitcase.

By the end of 1959 Hugo had signed out more than eighty NATO files and photographed several thousand pages of valuable economic and military information representing the highest classified categories. Between 1957 and 1960 members of the Politburo could read at their leisure the most confidential of NATO material thanks to the industry of the Canadian. Hugo never thought that the physical removal of documents represented great personal danger, the security system of NATO being so perfunctory. By 1959 Hugo, by his own admission later, had been routinely questioned only twice by NATO guards as he left the premises. The real danger arose more from disgruntled Soviets who became defectors or Allied counter-intelligence agents who might discover the source of the leaks.

The higher the classification of the document the fewer the people who had access. The right to sign out files was limited to each *rapporteur* whose responsibility was for a number of countries under his jurisdiction. One might memorize or take notes of certain individual sheets while in the office, as Hugo often did. But this was complicated and time-consuming. It was better to remove the documents from the registry at the end of the working day, take them home and return them the next morning. Sometimes a single document within the file would have as many as fifty sheets, which meant that Hugo sometimes stayed up almost all night photographing.

Upstairs in his closet in his chalet in Orsay he had perfected his photographic art. A small floodlight, a table with a stand on which to place the pages, were all the equipment he needed. In the late 1950s Xerox machines were not in common use, and a small cassette of thirty-five-millimetre film was by far the simplest method to transfer intelligence. Also, a film cassette could be hidden without difficulty.

If Hugo were to be caught in France, the French government would act with severity. The death penalty by guillotine could be requested. Other NATO countries could also charge the Canadian. And in the last analysis, Canada could ask for extradition and prosecution.

With his inventive mind Hugo created numerous cover stories if he should be caught. Whether he would be nimble enough to hide his tracks depended on his ingenuity. The NATO years were personally the most dangerous. If he carried out his KGB assignments for Paul, he had to have a fierce loyalty to the Russian. If Hugo was willing to risk his personal liberty or his life for some higher idealism that he passionately felt, it was a well-kept secret, deep in his most inner self. He has always strenuously denied being motivated by any lofty principles, but whatever he felt was felt deeply with conviction. But Hugo's daring was almost reckless, uncharacteristic of the fastidious academic, and displayed a courage never wholly apparent in the character exhibited to the outside world. About this time Hugo created the fanciful conception of a fellow agent that he wove into the fabric of his life and preserved for the future. In Canada this man would become Jacques La Liberté, in France he would be called Jean Masson and Pedro Garcia. Hugo could describe these people in minute detail, which he actually did on several occasions. The truth of these creations may be locked forever in Hugo's mind.

Jean Masson, the French intelligence agent, was described as a man in his late thirties in 1960, of medium build, about five feet seven inches in height, with black hair and a swarthy complexion. Masson's job, as an experienced agent, was to feed back to the Soviets misinformation through the "doctored" NATO files. The meetings with Masson were supposedly held mainly at NATO headquarters and once at the Grand Hotel in Paris in 1959. The type of material fed to the Russians would be left largely to Hugo's discretion. Masson permitted Hugo to remove eight out of every ten documents from NATO and photograph those of Hugo's own choosing. But the French agent was conversant with everything the Canadian did. Hugo said that after some years he was passed on to a Canadian handler substituting for Masson—Jacques La Liberté. No one was aware of La Liberté's existence except Hugo himself. But these men were made of faint images that danced away whenever anyone tried to come to grips with them. Once in a Paris bookstore Hugo apparently met by accident an ageing Spaniard, a veteran of the Spanish civil war whom he had engaged in conversation in his native tongue. The Spaniard's name may very well have been Pedro Garcia. Another chance meeting followed, and then a conversation outside a tiny bistro over a sidewalk table. Later, Pedro Garcia would be born again in Hugo's imagination and transformed into a secret agent of the West whose mission had become the direction of the Canadian in his double-agent life. But the world of espionage, as Hugo learned, had only one complete truth: deceit. A burnt-out spy was shown no mercy by either side; each disowned him. Hugo's defence lawyers later would base their arguments on the existence of these invisible men. But none—Masson, La Liberté, Garcia—ever came forward to identify themselves. If they had, if only one of them had, they could have saved Hugo.

Near the Place du Colonel Fabien in the nineteenth district close to the Communist party headquarters Hugo had been shown a dead-letter drop. It was a mailbox of the last resort, to be used only in extreme emergency. The box was hidden behind a loose brick in the wall of an apartment building. If Hugo should receive by radio the message that he was under surveillance, he must go immediately to the Place du Colonel Fabien. In the box he would find a new passport and instructions to proceed to Vienna to a prearranged meeting in the Hochstadtplatz. There, friends would make themselves known and take him across the Austrian border into Czechoslovakia and thence to the safety of Russia.

Defection was the final solution. But in his NATO days in Paris this idea was the furthest from Hugo's mind. Everything was going well. He was brimming with confidence and rather satisfied with himself. In all respects the outward signs of the Canadian's living style were unaltered. His simple habits and frugal personal needs never seemed to alter from year to year. Once in a while he might have a fling with an Oriental woman. But this was done so discreetly that it attracted little attention from any of his NATO colleagues. His life to outsiders seemed unchanged except for his impending divorce from Thérèse in 1959, and his proposed marriage to Fiorella. (Ironically Hugo had become a Catholic to wed Thérèse. But Thérèse before her divorce had left the Church, and Hugo remained Catholic.)

Hugo corresponded regularly with his mother and sister in Ottawa and sometimes with me in Montreal. He performed his duties at NATO conscientiously and left no room for complaint.

For the KGB, things seemed to be going well, too, although Hugo speculated that the burly and silent man who sometimes accompanied Paul to a rendezvous was a bodyguard and that on these days particularly the Russian acted in a more suspicious manner. But he was never certain there was danger. Paul rarely spoke about the problems that troubled him, and he behaved as if he didn't have a care in the world.

Often from the Gambetta métro Hugo and Paul would walk together through this working-class district to the Boulevard Menilmontant, alongside the sprawling Père La Chaise cemetery. On one side they would be flanked by the depressing tombstones and on the other by the wide boulevard. It was a quiet area in the evening where business could be discussed in total privacy. Paul would then decide to phone some fine restaurant whose number he would look up in his notebook, and if it wasn't too crowded, they would dine there. When Paul came by car, it was invariably driven by the bodyguard.

After four years Hugo had dined with Paul on countless evenings, in the best restaurants, drunk wine late into the night, and sometimes in a rare moment shared an intimate detail or two of Paul's private life. He owned a lovely Dacha on the Black Sea, hinting sometimes, after a bottle of wine, that one day Hugo might visit him there. Paul's presence gave Hugo confidence, often when he needed it most. However, regardless of the outward display of friendliness the Russian was a hard professional KGB officer. His duty to the organization came before all else. He wanted results and knew how to handle the Canadian so those results would be forthcoming.

In 1959 Hugo remarried. The following year Fiorella bore him his first son. From the beginning of the marriage, Fiorella was alone a great deal. She failed to understand why her husband spent so many evenings away from home or why he would disappear into the small room on the upper floor of their home in Orsay, photographing sheets of paper for hours at a time. All Hugo would say was that his photography was an essential part of his work. But he promised that in a year he would lead a more normal life because he was planning to leave NATO and continue his education in London. After his marriage Hugo had decided to end his career as a Soviet agent quietly and on good terms with the Russians. He was confident that his friend Paul would be sympathetic.

Hugo genuinely desired to return to the academic life, which was his first love. He had been lucky and had so far escaped detection by Russian defectors and Allied security, and he did not wish to push his luck too far. The word had quietly spread through the corridors of the NATO Secretariat that somewhere in the huge organization there lurked one or more traitors. Allied intelligence knew that vital documents had been passed on to the Russians. With the added insistence of his wife, Hugo decided it was time to leave Paris.

For the time being, however, he didn't divulge his plans to his NATO employers or the Russians. He realized he was too valuable a source of information for Paul to give up willingly without providing a good reason for his decision to resign from the alliance. He therefore invented a reason that he believed could solve the dilemma.

Meanwhile, Fiorella was growing increasingly unhappy. She came from a close-knit Italian family and resented the meetings and journeys of her husband from which she was excluded. To make matters worse, Hugo had to explain to his newly wed wife that he would shortly be flying to Cuba. He had been asked to prepare an economic development plan for that country with his former professor at the Sorbonne, S. Bettleheim, who had requested him. Bettleheim spoke no Spanish, a language Hugo spoke and wrote fluently. Upon his return from Cuba, he intended to notify Paul of his intentions to leave the organization. However, before the Canadian departed on his Cuban mission the family would holiday at Mariposa, his villa at Mijas, which had unexpectedly become available for a month.

From there the entire family would journey on to Ottawa, and he would subsequently leave for Cuba. Fiorella would wait at the Hambleton home on Ruskin for her husband to return.

The year 1960 was Hugo's most productive period for the KGB at NATO—a fact that could be verified by the frequency with which his name appeared on the NATO control sheets required for the signing out of documents. By his own admission he photographed thousands of classified items. Moscow was also keeping him busy by broadcasting uninterruptedly every week. Sometimes the messages were absurd and ordered impossible tasks. In late December a communication was received wishing Hugo a happy New Year. Another message read: "What policy should the USSR adopt toward NATO?" To this latter request Hugo replied in detail. This was the kind of working report he enjoyed doing because he believed he was influencing the fate of nations. Hugo's thoughtful ten-page reply to this latter Russian request was dropped off one Friday night in the Père La Chaise cemetery. He left the papers tucked in the grass behind a certain tombstone of a man who had died fifty years ago.

The Canadian had grown expert at receiving and deciphering the Russian codes. Fiorella had little or no idea why her husband spent so much time absorbed in his shortwave radio receiver at certain hours of the evening. But she didn't know much about radios, and Hugo played with his set like an engrossed child. As the years passed, she became more than vaguely suspicious of her husband's unusual activities, but it is only fair to say she did not understand until the very end the real nature of his work.

In the late summer of 1960 Hugo took his annual leave, travelling as planned first to Spain and then to Ottawa with his wife and son. From Ottawa Hugo proceeded alone to Mexico City where he spent several days visiting old friends before flying to Havana, where he arrived on September 11. He stayed in Cuba for three weeks, helping the new revolutionary government of Fidel Castro to initiate an economic program of reform that would make the country less dependent on sugar production.

While in Havana he appeared on a number of television programs, and was given a luxury suite at the Havana Riviera Hotel, where he joined Professor Bettleheim. The two men were given every facility to travel throughout the country, examining the industrial potential and preparing recommendations for a five-year economic recovery program, concentrating on agrarian reform. This was an important period for Castro and particularly the West when the lines of communication were still open with the United States. But Russia was beginning to make generous offers to Cuba. Whoever could offer the most help, the most intelligent and astute direction, would have a chance to impose its policy on Cuba and hence win an ally in a strategic region of the world.

Perhaps it was a coincidence that Hugo, a knowledgeable student of Latin American affairs, should arrive in Cuba at this crucial juncture. It is more than likely that he had a mission to perform, one of attempting to gather intelligence and assist the Russians in formulating their successful proposals that joined Castro with the Communists. This would not be the last time that the Canadian would arrive on the scene during a period of revolutionary change in Latin America when the Soviets were seeking to secure a position of authority and influence.

After three weeks Hugo returned to Ottawa and then flew his family back to France, arriving in Paris on October 14. He spent a short while perfecting a thirty-page report on the agrarian reform movement. Hugo claimed he gave the paper to John Licence, his superior at NATO. But he also admitted he transferred a copy to Paul. A week later he received a radio message from Moscow warmly congratulating him on the considerable value of his study.

It was in late October of 1960 that Hugo made up his mind to definitely quit NATO. He was in high standing with Moscow after his Cuban journey. Perhaps they would be in a favourable mood to understand his genuine desire to return to the academic world and would offer no resistance. Study was the one real love of his life that was clean, unsoiled and detached from the other subterranean world in which he dwelt. Not the least of Hugo's fears was the uncompromising position Paul could take if he chose. He might do more than exert the stern cautions of a big brother. Hugo was already deeply compromised. He must cleverly present his arguments for leaving NATO. The Russian was exceedingly shrewd and would quickly see through a thinly disguised ruse. Hugo decided to broach the subject at their next meeting.

His arguments were helped by the fact that in 1960 the Cold War between East and West had grown intense. Patriotic fever was running high in America. In some quarters it had reached a hysterical level. NATO became a logical target of suspicion. For the Russians it was important to preserve those people vital to their intelligence organization. Paul had indicated to Hugo at numerous meetings that his reports were valued and sometimes reached the Politburo level, and the conciseness and the studied comments that accompanied copies of the NATO documents brought high compliments. Hugo had to be protected.

"In Russia you could have a good life," Paul had once said. "You would not be the first Westerner who sought our hospitality."

In spite of his betrayal Hugo loved Canada. He did not honestly believe he had done anything to harm his native land, and he did not wish to exile himself from the country where he was born and where he had grown up. The thought of defection was repulsive to him. It would only be a desperate last resort in order to save himself from a much worse fate. One of the reasons Hugo was so safe in his department in NATO was largely due to his immediate superior, John Licence, who was involved in a minor homosexual scandal at about the same time that Hugo had decided to leave the organization. This automatically diverted attention away from Hugo, about whom there was no suspicion. Everyone held the Canadian in good regard. Furthermore and more important, NATO security considered Hugo clean. Therefore, when Hugo made known his intentions to leave NATO in order to attend the London School of Economics, he was informed by his superiors that he would be able to depart with favourable recommendations.

In early December of 1960 Hugo met with his KGB officer for dinner at one of Paul's favourite restaurants off the Boulevard St. Germain. It happened coincidentally that a radio request had been received by Hugo from Moscow that week asking for figures on enriched uranium production in France for the past year. This would involve removing and photographing some of the most sensitive information in the cosmic files. The Canadian protested for once at the naïveté of the instructions. The request was far too dangerous. Paul took a conciliatory approach and agreed. Ignore the message. This Hugo thought was a good omen and the right moment to tell Paul of his new plans. They were having an excellent dinner, the atmosphere was friendly, and Paul was in one of his best moods, cordial and eager to enjoy good conversation.

When the dinner was almost over, Hugo told the KGB officer of his wish to leave NATO and continue his studies. Hugo was thirty-seven years old, and if he didn't complete his doctorate in economics now, he probably never would. Then he spontaneously added another irrefutable argument for his departure, which he invented. He could fall under suspicion at NATO. He wasn't at the moment but because of the homosexual scandal involving his superior, Hugo could be investigated, and if that happened, questions could be asked about the files he had signed out. One might notice that they were always returned on the following day. Someone in security could decide to pursue the matter further.

"You always have the mailbox in Place du Colonel Fabien with the passport," Paul assured him calmly.

Hugo hastily added there could be little real evidence against him at the present. But if he continued to provide information at the same level for the KGB, he could soon be compromised. Better to leave earlier in safety than later under a cloud of suspicion.

"You are the best judge if there is any real evidence against you," Paul said. "But if there is, your transportation could be arranged. It is always available. Once you reach the East, you could make a public statement at a news conference about NATO." Paul was seriously concerned about the Canadian's safety. He did not want Hugo caught. Whatever the reasons, his feelings were genuine.

Hugo hastily declared the situation was not quite that serious. The imminent retirement of his chief, John Licence, would be the right moment for Hugo himself to depart inconspicuously for his studies in London. To Hugo's surprise Paul offered no resistance. He agreed that this was an exceptional opportunity to quietly slip out of the organization with honour and continue his academic career. If study was what Hugo really wanted, then nothing should stand in his way. Now was the time when the benefit of his NATO experience coupled with the marvellous atmosphere of the London School of Economics could profit Hugo enormously. Hugo must improve his position in the world as a man of influence, a scholar whose opinion would be respected by people in high places. Paul's motives were not purely altruistic. He, too, was thinking of the future. After dinner that evening they strolled casually down the Boulevard St. Germain and turned into a small side street that led past the antique shops of the Rue des Beaux Arts until they reached the Seine.

Here Paul said good-bye. There was a genuine feeling of affection in the farewell. Their paths would probably not cross again for a long while, but in the future it was possible that unknown events would draw them together once more. Whatever happened, wherever he might be, Paul promised the Canadian he would know of his progress. Meanwhile, he told Hugo to destroy immediately all evidence of his employment in the service of the KGB. All communications from Moscow would cease forthwith. Paul, the urbane KGB officer who enjoyed the good things the capitalist society of the West could provide, then shook hands with Hugo. He walked away, slowly disappearing in the dark evening mist that drifted along the banks of the river.

That night Hugo destroyed his camera. He short-circuited the radio receiver as he had been shown, and buried the set in a wooded area near his home in Orsay. Nothing compromising existed except for a few NATO documents that were of no great importance which he wished to keep for personal reference. Otherwise there was no incriminating evidence of his five faithful years of work for the KGB in NATO.

The next month, January 1961, Hugo visited Vienna where he met a KGB contact at a prearranged rendezvous in a coffee house off the Hochstadtplatz not far from the Communist party headquarters. The KGB might be the largest secret army in the world, but it certainly was not the most original. For fifteen years they would use the same system of clandestine signs and code words for recognition. A post near the Hochstadtplatz rendezvous would be marked with two chalked crosses. If the post was chalk-marked, it would indicate the meeting would take place. At the entrance to the coffee house, which served delicious Viennese torte, the Russian would approach Hugo with a password.

"You have some etchings in Paris for me?" the Russian would ask in English. Baggy trousers and an ill-fitting suit would frequently identify the awkward agent who behaved as though he had just stepped across the Czechoslovakian border at Bratislava.

"No, I have no etchings in Paris. But I have some in London," Hugo would reply. Sometimes London would be changed to Paris depending on which city he had come from.

With this clumsy exchange the parties would slip into the coffee house for further discussion over cake and coffee. Vienna was the last stop on the passage to the East. Perhaps on that journey in 1961 Hugo was testing the strength of his connections to make sure that the gateway to Russia remained open should the need arise. There was considerable KGB agent traffic both ways over the Czechoslovakian border, a short drive to Bratislava where a Soviet military airport had direct links with Moscow. It was a good feeling to know that the Viennese arrangement had not altered.

Although Hugo eventually made only one formal admission that he travelled to Russia through Vienna in 1975, there is strong evidence from his passport entries that on his three journeys to Vienna between 1960 and 1975 he went into Czechoslovakia through Bratislava with KGB officers, and was flown at least twice by Russian military transport to Moscow. The reason is obvious. In fifteen years the technical equipment of spying changed dramatically. It was safer and more efficient, given Hugo's ease of movement, to teach an important spy his duties where the equipment and teachers were readily available.

In 1961 before leaving Paris Hugo renewed his practical interest in Latin America and became involved in the Canadian Association for Latin American Studies. On occasion this association would meet in Cuba where Hugo developed his relationship with Ricardo Escantin of the SIM (Servicia de Intelligencia Militar) of Cuba, Castro's secret police. It is known that Escantin visited with Hugo later when he worked for the Canadian International Development Agency in Haiti. His involvement in the association along with his scholarly credentials earned him a warm reception in the academic and government circles of most Latin American countries.

As a Canadian who had every opportunity to make outstanding contributions to his nation, he stood at the crossroads of his career in 1961. For a few brief weeks during that year he struggled with the agonizing pain of self-doubt. If he wished, he could break away from the KGB, but this would require a massive effort of will. And beyond that, it would involve admissions, a stigma that would be forever attached to his character and result in a major personal dislocation. But Hugo did not find the tenacious grip of his masters that painful. Although much of the damage he had done was irreparable, it might be pardoned in a less hysterical period and at a future time. Canada was not the United States. If Hugo had confessed, he might have found his way out of the jungle of deceit and lies that he had wandered into. But that decision would have involved outright rejection of the Soviets, and he did not wish to alienate them. The heady atmosphere of surreptitious meetings, direct communication with Moscow centre, the dangerous double life, were stimulants.

He viewed himself as a world power broker, capable of secretly shifting the balance of power between Russia and the West. With greater clarity of mind, deeper wisdom, and maturity, he might have recognized that he was more a pawn than a broker.

- CHAPTER SIX -

The
Academic

Hugo's resignation letter to NATO was thoughtfully composed but verbose. It was addressed to André Vincent, his new superior, who had replaced Licence. He regretted the sad choice he must make, but his desire to continue his academic career had won out over his wish to become an international civil servant. The employment had given so much in the way of fruitful, practical experience that it would always be of great benefit. No one at NATO objected to the argument that he wished to pursue his studies. The idea was commendable. The hope was expressed that Hugo might one day consider returning to NATO. But he had no such wish. He was happy to see the last of the organization and was looking forward with pleasure to living in London, although that city would be no more than a base.

Before Hugo left Paris, rumours had grown rife about the homosexual ring and threats of blackmail in high places that could put NATO security at risk. It is conceivable the KGB itself had promoted the rumours to cause distraction at a time when their important agent was leaving. Hardly anyone noticed Hugo's departure. But his five years of espionage had grievously damaged the Allies. The sheer volume, variety and sensitivity of much of the material he photographed would give experienced Soviet intelligence officers a comprehensive picture of the North Atlantic Treaty Organization with all its weaknesses and strengths for years to come. Many of its future policies could be predicted.

When Hugo moved his residence to London for the first year of his doctorate, he gave an almost audible gasp of relief. The pressure was off at last. The protective environment of the academic world would be greatly relaxing, like slipping into the warm waters of a calm and peaceful sea.

1961 - 1964

The next three years were a time of partial rest from the tension and excitement of the preceding years. In his first blissful season as a student Hugo returned often to Paris. He forgot about the fake passport left for him behind the loose bricks in the wall of an apartment building near Place du Colonel Fabien. That belonged to remote events that happened on another planet. Distantly he wondered whether it was still there and dimly recalled his instructions if the urgent need for him to defect arose. His life was transformed, emerging from the dark chrysalis in which he had lived to a bright forum of lectures, debates, and provocative intellectual discussions. The joy of study, the pleasant philosophical bantering, the radical student fervour that swept through the corridors of the university were enormously stimulating.

But something was still missing in Hugo's life. His marriage to the passive Fiorella did nothing to subdue the urge he had for excitement. Now and then he became anxious, more unsettled, as if a secret longing was nagging at his soul. The truth was that his present life did nothing to satisfy the craving for the dark, mysterious experiences he had left behind. But he need have had no fear. The KGB had already planned his life. No matter in what direction he chose to go, they would be waiting for him, ready to guide him. The appointment had long ago been made.

Hugo always had the capacity and the remarkable concentration to apply himself with passion to his studies. No matter what external pressures were applied, no matter the distractions, he was able to concentrate on his work, filling his quota of assignments, attending lectures and preparing voluminous notes for his thesis. But he had freedom. He could travel.

He had sufficient money. Some had come from the Russians before he left Paris—about two thousand dollars—his mother supplied additional funds, and he had some NATO savings. His Madrid apartment brought in only a small sum, as did his beautiful villa, Mariposa. The villa was cradled on a cliff in the hills of Mijas where one had a view of the sea and Marbella from a magnificent terrace. Mariposa was a small paradise which sat like a jewel in a forest of pine trees and wild flowers. His real estate agent in Malaga continued to be responsible for the management of the properties, somehow constantly renting the villa at a ridiculously low figure and controlling the right of use and most of the revenue. All the Canadian could do was use the villa between tenants, sometimes alone and sometimes in the company of his family.

Since Hugo's thesis for his doctorate dealt with Spain, he travelled there frequently. The small apartment Bessie purchased in Torremolinos was vacant more often than the villa, and he would spend rare weeks there, relishing each day. That summer of 1961, Bessie arrived in Paris to accompany Hugo to Spain. Fiorella, who was not fond of Bessie, although they had met only once in Ottawa, did not make the journey to Torremolinos that year. Hugo had looked forward to his mother's visit; she was the one person in the world who understood him and accepted him as he was. In the autumn they travelled to the famous Library of Simancas in the north of the country to do some of his research on sixteenth-century Spain. Bessie, in her own right an able historian, gave Hugo much useful advice. But the advice was not only academic. It ranged over many subjects, including her son's past life in NATO, and the course his future should take, much to the chagrin of Fiorella. No love was lost between the two women. Any female in Hugo's life constituted a threat to Bessie, and she was as ruthless as she was powerful in crushing any opposition to the still unfulfilled ambitions she held for her son. She was determined that nothing and no one should stand in Hugo's way.

Hugo had not contacted any Russians for over a year and believed that they had decided to give him up since he could no longer be of service to them. But in 1962 Vladimir Borodin without notice visited him and Fiorella in Torremolinos. Borodin was attached at the time to the Russian embassy in Amsterdam, but on a journey some months previously through Ottawa had spoken to Bessie. She had given him the address of her son.

"How do you enjoy your life as a student?" Borodin asked innocently among other questions.

Hugo replied that he enjoyed his studies very much and politely inquired after Paul. Paul was away for a long period on important business, he was told. However, if Hugo had any need to speak to someone, the system of the métro rendezvous in Paris could always be reactivated. He could not for the time being meet his old friend Paul, but another KGB officer—simply known as Paul Two—would always be available any time Hugo passed through Paris. If the métro meetings were inconvenient, the letter drop in the mailbox at Place du Colonel Fabien could be used, as well as the one behind the tombstone in the cemetery at Père La Chaise. Borodin was not persistent, but he was very friendly. Acting on instructions, he was anxious to please Hugo. The KGB wished, at all costs, to keep the connection alive.

Over the next few years, Hugo relished the freedom of England, the speeches of Hyde Park Corner on a Sunday and, above all, the vast storehouse of knowledge and art preserved in the vaults of the British Museum where he spent a great deal of time. The British Museum, of which he was an associate, played a large role in Hugo's research. It became a kind of second home.

Hugo saw an agent who substituted for Paul on his visits through Paris. This KGB official was much different from the man he replaced, but pleasing nevertheless. Never once in the three years of infrequent passage through Paris were matters of espionage discussed. The lunches and dinners, the theatre performances they attended, were social events. Only once during his London years did he meet with his old friend.

Paul showed up on a day in August of 1963. They met in a Parisian restaurant when Hugo was en route to Torremolinos. Arrangements had been made previously by a letter received from East Berlin. When he arrived at the restaurant close to the Palais Chaillot, Paul was waiting for him. He said he had made a special trip to see his Canadian friend. They respected each other, had worked together sometimes under difficult conditions and shared a common danger. They knew many of the secrets that had shaped both their lives. That evening they would simply celebrate. No business would be discussed.

Both men would be relaxed and enjoy the good fortune that had brought them together in Paris again. In the comfortable atmosphere of the restaurant Hugo saw Paul as a human being rather than as a man whose efficiency could be ruthless and mechanical. There were deep human qualities in the Russian that Hugo could genuinely understand. In Moscow Paul had a family, he had friends and held a high position in the bureaucratic system of his country. Their relationship now was informal, one of two equals meeting to have a good time.

"Tonight," Paul insisted, "we will go to the Bal Tabarin and see the girls and enjoy ourselves for a change. No work."

Hugo objected. He was anxious to go on to Spain that evening to finish the last of the research on his thesis. The deadline for the completion of his work on the economic decline of Spain in the sixteenth century was drawing near. But Paul refused to hear Hugo's protests.

"Tonight you are my guest." Paul was adamant.

By the time dinner ended, Hugo's resistance had crumbled. Maybe they could be friends on a new basis. Or was this Paul's way of saying good-bye? But the KGB never said good-bye, or if they did, it was a final farewell. There was nothing in between. Only when one grew too old to be of further service did they leave you alone.

The Russian's warm comradeliness was flattering. Perhaps the attention was a prelude to some new request. But Hugo had made his position clear at their last meeting, and it had been accepted. It was, however, conceivable, he conjectured, that the KGB officer was testing the strength of the relationship. Was it durable.? Certainly Hugo could not be of help now to his friend. He was forty-one years old. A mature student. He would soon have another degree from the London School of Economics. He belonged in the halls of a university, not in the conspiratorial and devious world of espionage. But Hugo knew too much about the Russians, the KGB operators in Paris, Vienna, Ottawa and London. His radio receiver codes, chemically treated writing pads, had, according to Hugo, been destroyed. But Paul only had Hugo's word for that.

Paul had a mission to perform that night, as Hugo would later learn. How that night would end depended on the conclusion he reached. His manner and friendliness were designed to that end. He wanted Hugo to talk. He wanted to discover whether the Canadian had altered his loyalty to the KGB and could be a danger to the organization. If at the end of the evening he was convinced that Hugo could be of further service, they would shake hands and wish each other *au revoir*. If Paul came to the reluctant conclusion that the Canadian could turn against the Soviets, however, there was a different kind of farewell in store. In his breast pocket the KGB officer carried a stainless-steel pen-gun that held a single cartridge in readiness. The poison-tipped projectile was the size of a minute ball-bearing. When discharged a foot or less away from its victim, the projectile had the capacity to penetrate through a layer of clothing. The tiny pellet contained nicin with some aneroid bacteria sealed by wax in two miniscule holes. Body heat would melt the wax when it was imbedded beneath the skin. The highly toxic poison, several times the strength of a viper's venom, was fatal. The pen-gun was standard KGB equipment. In 1978 Georgi Markov, a Bulgarian émigré, was assassinated in the middle of the afternoon on London's crowded Bond Street by a similar method—a pellet fired from an umbrella.

Hugo and Paul had a fine dinner together. They drank vintage champagne and dined on oysters, sole meunière and a dazzling, flaming dessert. They caught the late night show at the Bal Tabarin as Paul arranged and picked up two women in the night club who turned out to be attractive, expensive prostitutes. The men were both more than slightly drunk by the time the show ended. One of the prostitutes fondled the Russian while the other began to stroke Hugo at their night club table. Paul was an astute man, drunk or sober. There were certain qualities in Hugo that he could easily exploit: the craving for excitement, the dependency that had developed between them. Yet Paul harboured a number of reservations about the weaknesses he had found in Hugo's character. The Canadian was tightlipped but, when forced to give an explanation, he talked too much. Paul was not sure how his man would react if extreme pressure was brought to bear. Yet Hugo had demonstrated his loyalty in the risks he had already taken for the KGB, and there was no doubt that his allegiance to the organization would not change.

"You are a good comrade," Paul blurted out that evening at the night club. Paul had huge bearlike hands, and one thumped Hugo playfully on the back.

"I am not a comrade. I don't think I could be one," Hugo snapped, contradicting Paul with the help of the alcohol. Something in the patrician image Hugo held of himself rebelled at the idea of being a comrade. "But I could be part of the KGB officer cadre."

The prostitutes paid no attention to the men's conversation. Political beliefs were irrelevant. They wanted to get on with their business, be paid and complete their night's work as quickly as possible.

"I shall recommend you to become an officer," Paul promised. "You are highly thought of and respected by my superiors."

That evening at the night club Paul told Hugo that he had been born in a small village in the Ukraine and had fought as a partisan against the Germans in World War II. Because his father had been a good Communist and one of the managers of agriculture production in the Ukraine, Paul had been permitted to attend the officer-cadet training school in Leningrad where he distinguished himself by winning academic honours. He was found to have an unusual aptitude for organization and languages and was recommended for the special intelligence army school in Moscow where the officers are trained for the GRU, the military equivalent of the KGB. After service in Soviet agencies in various parts of the world, including London, Washington and

Paris, Paul was finally transferred to the Soviet espionage service. It was obvious he was an important person, a colonel or higher with considerable authority. Hugo seemed to be his very special responsibility.

Back in Russia, Hugo learned, Paul's wife complained constantly at his long absences. He missed very much his three children whom he seldom saw. Although he had a fierce attachment to the service that employed him and would always obey their orders, he confided to Hugo that the delightful pleasures of Paris and Vienna had spoiled him forever.

At the end of the evening, the men embraced each other like brothers, swearing eternal friendship. They then went their separate ways with the prostitutes in tow to complete the evening's revelry. Paul had not forgotten the deadly fountain pen in his breast pocket. But Hugo was a good comrade, loyal and trusted. Paul could never bring himself to harm the Canadian. Anyone who would suggest such a deed must be mad.

The next day Hugo completed his journey to Torremolinos and his family.

During his years at the London School of Economics, Hugo applied himself fully to his studies. Upon graduation at the age of forty-three he would be among the oldest students receiving a Ph.D. He studied at an age when most academics had secured tenure in universities and were well launched on their careers. It took dedication and singleness of purpose to pursue his goals.

He now had two children and a none-too-stable marriage to contend with. His wife was unhappy with his philanderings. Fiorella had married Hugo as an established economist with a good NATO job, only to find herself with two children living with an unemployed academic. Her growing suspicion of Hugo's other life deeply disturbed their marital relationship. Also, her mother-in-law's attentiveness to her husband was difficult for Fiorella to countenance.

Before the year 1964 ended there were a few bright and happy weeks of reunion when Bessie joined her son in London. She was always an anchor of sanity who helped to put in proportion the complications in her son's personal life. Bessie was seventy-five years old then, but one would hardly notice her age. She looked and acted twenty-five years younger. To the acute annoyance of his wife, Hugo left London with his mother to enjoy a short delightful holiday in their Torremolinos apartment. This act further deepened the rift in the already shaky marriage.

In the spring of 1964 Hugo's doctoral thesis was accepted by the London School of Economics with honours, and the Canadian set about finding employment as an economist. He had no desire to return to NATO. And even if he wished, after his resignation and the shadow of scandal that had clouded the career of John Licence, it would be unwise to work there. Hugo wrote letters seeking employment at twenty Canadian universities, including three in Quebec. Meanwhile he contacted his old friend Lloyd Delameter in Paris. Delameter was now running a successful school for American students. During the summer of 1964 Hugo was employed there as an assistant.

The first favourable reply Hugo received to his job applications was from Laval University in Quebec City. Employment as one of the few English Canadians at this predominantly French institution appealed to him very much. It offered him seclusion and, paradoxically, the anonymity he always sought.

- CHAPTER SEVEN -

The
Colonel

1965 - 1972

Rudolph Herrmann was born seven years after Hugh George Hambleton, and their paths were to frequently cross in out-of-the-way places around the world.

Herrmann, whose real name may have been Ludek Zemenak, was a dedicated Communist recruited into the world of espionage in the early 1950s after distinguishing himself at the University of Prague in international affairs. After a short spell of military service he was chosen by KGB scouts for training in that organization. The KGB infiltrated Herrmann from East Germany into West Germany in 1960. They even supplied an acceptable wife named Inga who suited him perfectly.

The two of them settled comfortably in the town of Heilbronn in Germany where the former Czech opened a camera shop. Throughout the years the KGB nourished this agent with money and directives, establishing him as a solid West German citizen. In 1962 a son who would grow up in Canada was born to the couple in Germany. With his background established and with unquestionable credentials at his command, he was now ready for the important role the KGB had conceived for him from the beginning. The KGB agent studied English and applied to emigrate to Canada. Immigration to Canada in the 1960s was easy for a West German, and Herrmann found no difficulty in having his application approved by the Canadian immigration authorities in Frankfurt. With the proceeds of the sale of the camera shop, supplemented by sufficient KGB funds, and with secret cipher pads and radio equipment to facilitate shortwave reception from Moscow, the immigrant departed with his wife and child in the early winter of 1962 for Toronto. On arrival Herrmann purchased a delicatessen near the Canadian Broadcasting Corporation offices on Jarvis Street in that city.

As a KGB captain the spy made no substantial contribution to his organization. In the first few years of his career, he achieved very little except to establish himself in America as a trusted link with important North American agents. The KGB were in no great hurry. Herrmann led the normal life of a small businessman in Toronto, raising two children like other Canadians, and being accepted as a family of good citizens. In Toronto, Rudi's delicatessen became a meeting place for pro-German gatherings. Patrons from the Toronto German-Canadian Association came to spend time with the Herrmanns and to eat the wife's good German cooking. Shortly thereafter, Herrmann, an extremely versatile and intelligent man, decided to become a producer of commercial advertising films. He had the adaptability to turn his hand to almost anything he wished.

In 1964 the KGB recalled their man to Vienna, and there his function in America was more fully explained. He would become the master coordinator of the North American Soviet spy network. He was then given the names of all his key contacts, the most valuable and trusted. One of the names Moscow gave him was that of Professor Hambleton, who could be found on the staff of Laval University in Quebec City.

By the time the two men met, both had spent roughly the same period working for the KGB, but Hugo's contribution had been of infinitely greater value to the Soviet intelligence service.

Hugo was happy to be back in Canada. He began teaching at Laval in 1965 and honestly felt that maybe at last he would settle down to an academic life with prospects of recognition and secure employment. He rented a modest two-bedroom apartment at 2455 Chemin St. Foy. He was rather amused to discover that one of his neighbours was a Parti Québécois activist who one day would become a minister in the Cabinet of Premier René Lévesque. Hugo bought a few pieces of cheap living room furniture, two beds, some kitchen equipment and a large dining room table that would become a massive desk laden with his books and university papers. On the wall he hung a small sketch by A.Y. Jackson that had belonged to his mother and, with his customary application to detail, settled down to his new career with his wife and two children.

He soon discovered that he had inadvertently kept one yellow KGB notebook that contained some compromising details of meetings with Paul in Europe. He put the notebook in a file in his Laval office and promptly forgot about it. He placed his recently acquired Grundig shortwave receiver in a prominent position on the bedroom dresser. A shortwave receiver continued to be a permanent part of Hugo's life, and he listened to broadcasts in French, Spanish, Italian and German at odd times of the day or night to the annoyance of his wife.

His working and sleeping habits were unpredictable, but he always managed to complete his university duties satisfactorily. He minded his own business at Laval and was amicable to those around him. Staff and students liked the quiet, modest professor. He displayed a great tolerance toward his students, going so far as to give them, in advance of the exams, questions that he intended to ask. This endeared him to his pupils. The atmosphere at Laval was much to his liking, and Hugo adapted to a lifestyle that suited his temperament admirably. None of Hugo's neighbours at his apartment on St. Foy exchanged a word with him. He fraternized with few of his university associates and carried out his assignments efficiently and without undue attention.

From the first day as a member of the staff at Laval, Hugo earned the reputation of an excellent, conscientious academic. Within six months of his appointment he vanished from the outside world without a noticeable ripple, to become a grey, unspectacular scholar among the thousands of students and hundreds of professors who populated the concrete halls and innumerable classrooms of this huge Quebec university.

More than a year had passed since he had last heard from any of his KGB friends. He didn't miss them particularly. Fiorella was happier, too. Yet now and then, Hugo had a twinge of hunger for the old feeling of excitement that had added adventure and importance to his life. In Canada, life was good, the university routine undeviating, but Quebec City was dull. It wasn't Paris or London. He desperately yearned to travel, to visit some of the old European haunts, yet his career was taking him in other directions. His position at the university was a platform from which he could become a man of influence, not in Europe but in Latin America.

Hugo had been allotted a small mezzanine office above the main corridor with his name *H.G. Hambleton* printed on a plaque on the door. In 1967, toward the end of the school term, the professor was preoccupied with examinations and his summer vacation. He had little time to think about anything except his busy schedule; all other things had been thrust temporarily from his mind. Perhaps everything might have remained that way except for the quiet and unexpected knock on his office door in early April of that year.

Hugo was busy marking examination papers when the door to his tiny office opened slowly and a broad-shouldered, powerfully built man stood at the entrance. Hugo had never seen him before but some infallible instinct told him that the stranger who filled the doorway came from his other life, which he could never shed. The man slipped over the threshold without an invitation and closed the door silently. He carried a small executive-type briefcase and wore a light tan coat. He could have been an alert, aggressive business executive. His manner was polite but forthright. A widow's peak of black hair, trimmed short and brushed down neatly, somehow accented the rather wide cheekbones. Hugo had seen many of these Slavic faces before. But he was surprised at the stranger's initial remarks.

"Professor Hambleton, I have been looking for you," the man began.

Hugo nodded uncertainly. There was hardly a need to look for him. His name-plate was on the door, and his phone number and address were in the Quebec telephone directory. He doubted whether anyone had to search very hard to find him. He was the only Hambleton listed in the phone book.

The slight accent was definitely not Russian, but was from one of the Slavic countries. His English was almost perfectly fluent, precise and clearly learned. Hugo put down the black pencil with which he marked the exam papers.

"My name is Rudi Herrmann," the stranger said. "I'm a motion picture director and producer who has done some work recently for the CBC and collaborated on a few political campaign films for the Liberal party. I have a problem with which you may be able to help." What Herrmann said was the truth. He had worked for a Toronto advertising agency that had produced a political campaign documentary for the Liberal party.

"You could have phoned," Hugo replied, a little annoyed at the unannounced intrusion. He thought his initial impression of the man could be wrong, but he wasn't sure. They had to talk first. Herrmann would be slow to commit himself if Hugo's appraisal was correct.

"I'm really sorry to intrude this way, Professor Hambleton. I tried to reach you at home several times, but I couldn't."

Hugo had been away for several days, and his wife and children were in Ottawa. He had only returned late last night. It was almost impossible to reach him by telephone at his office because he was always in class. He only came here to spend time at the end of each day. Herrmann would have to know that. He could have watched the professor's movements, waiting for the hour when he would be alone. But that elaborate precaution was unnecessary. All day long the corridors of the university were usually thronging with students either coming or going to classes. People hardly noticed Hugo. And no one would be interested in Herrmann.

Herrmann said agreeably, "Wouldn't it be better to discuss the reason for my visit somewhere else. We might be disturbed here."

Hugo deliberated for a moment. The man seemed reasonable and charming. But he was very busy. Why did he have to leave his office?

"We could have a cup of coffee in the university cafeteria," Hugo said.

Hugo knew that no KGB agent would agree to talk business in the confines of a private office he had never visited before. He would be wary, choosing to talk in a crowded public place in preference to the privacy of an unknown one. Herrmann quickly accepted the invitation to go to the university cafeteria.

"Be my guest," Herrmann said amiably.

No one paid much attention to the two men walking into the busy cafeteria. Once or twice a student might have glanced curiously at Herrmann speaking English, but often Professor Hambleton entertained English guests, so this was not too unusual.

"Are you making a film about Quebec?" Hugo asked casually.

"The political aspect of the film is what I have come to discuss. The film will be about the life of the late Premier Duplessis."

Strange, Hugo thought, that a foreigner should be interested in Duplessis, who had ruled Quebec with the authority of a dictator a quarter of a century ago. Why should this man of obviously Slavic descent have such a keen sense of Canadian political history, especially when Duplessis reigned so long ago? Then another idea alerted him: Duplessis had outlawed the Communist party and instituted the infamous Padlock Law, which allowed his government to padlock any establishment that in his opinion published subversive literature. The premier had used the law to silence his opposition. Herrmann's next remarks put Hugo on guard.

"The film will have wide distribution in North America."

Then he added, "and I hope Europe as well. I have excellent contacts in Europe."

"Where in Europe?" Hugo asked cautiously.

"Many cities," Herrmann replied, "but especially London, Paris and Vienna. But now I require a consultant who knows Quebec and has the kind of background you have."

Herrmann showed Hugo a résumé of his achievements. They were impressive. He had produced a dozen documentaries for large corporations. He had become a landed Canadian immigrant in 1963 and would soon become a Canadian citizen. Herrmann elaborated on his background in Czechoslovakia and on his emigration from West Germany to Toronto. Hugo listened without comment. An appointment was made to meet that evening for dinner in the cafeteria of the Château Frontenac hotel to discuss further the terms under which Herrmann would employ Hugo as a consultant. Herrmann's last word before he departed was that they might have some friends in common.

They met for dinner as agreed. Hugo chose a table near the window overlooking the terrace. But Herrmann was not satisfied with the choice and decided upon another table in the centre of the room. At that moment Hugo realized the inescapable truth. The technique was recognizable. This move was a security precaution. If he had had doubts that afternoon, he had none now.

When they were seated and served, Herrmann said, "Our common friend is Paul."

Hugo shivered slightly. Not in fear but in relief that the years of expectation had come to an end. The long wait was over. They had found him again.

If Hugo's surmise was correct, Herrmann had come to deliver instructions. But Herrmann was no Paul. Their characters and manners were vastly different. Furthermore, circumstances had drastically altered. Hugo no longer worked in the heart of an organization that had vital information about Western economic and military resources. He was a professor at a university and did not yet have influence or a position that could help shape public opinion.

By the time the meeeting ended, the professor's role had been made clear and accepted. He would gather information on military and political matters in a general way relating to Canada. Meanwhile he should make an effort to grow closer to the Canadian political scene. Politics, standing up before gatherings, was abhorrent to his nature. He could think of nothing less

appealing. Herrmann made no reference to the film about
Duplessis that he had mentioned that afternoon.

A few weeks later Herrmann visited Hugo again and made a
specific but curious request. He asked for information about the
activities of the Communist government of the People's Republic
of China. Hugo simply wrote the Chinese nationalist embassy in
Ottawa and in reply received more than two dozen pages on the
activities of the Chinese Communists. He summarized them and
passed on the information to Herrmann a month later.

If the professor was a part-time spy, Herrmann acted as
though he were a largely unemployed officer with an important
title who spent most of his time making films. He could travel
freely without suspicion as a motion picture director-producer. In
1967 he had been promoted to the rank of colonel in the KGB.

The next year Herrmann applied for a U.S. visa and moved
with his family to a home in a New York suburb, leaving his
oldest son Peter behind as a student studying architecture at
McGill University in Montreal

Hugo's loyalty to the KGB, implanted long ago, was like a
glowing ember that had never died. The meeting at the Château
Frontenac had rekindled the flame and started a friendship with
Herrmann—if one could call it that—which would last for almost
ten years. Hugo, Herrmann and Paul would all age together in
the service of the KGB. But each of the three men was destined to
end his career in a markedly different manner.

Early in 1968, by means of a phone call Herrmann notified
Hugo of an impending rendezvous that he must attend. Two men
whom he had never seen before awaited him in front of the
Ottawa post office outside the main entrance. When he arrived,
he was conducted a short distance to a parked car on Wellington
Street. The instructions he received that day dealt with the dead-
letter drops where he could deposit his reports. One drop was
known as "the hunting lodge" and the other as "the fishing
lodge." They were approximately twenty-five miles from
Montreal on the road to Ottawa.

Hugo enquired after his old contact Vladimir Borodin, who
had recruited him twenty years earlier. But these new, young KGB
men who met Hugo outside the post office had never heard of
Borodin. They were businesslike, ruthless. They had been ordered to pass on the location of the drops, which they did with
clearly drawn diagrams, and when they had finished their
business, Hugo left the vehicle which had cruised down Elgin
Street and stopped not far from his mother's house on Ruskin

Avenue. The clandestine nature of the meeting in Ottawa represented to Hugo the absurd lengths to which Russians would go to preserve secrecy about many unimportant matters. But he was used to the Soviets, and this furtive behaviour didn't surprise him.

When he later visited the lodges for the drops, he was astounded at what he saw. The lodges were dilapidated buildings with broken windows nailed up with boards, doors hanging off their hinges. Both houses were deserted, derelict, and obviously had been left that way for many years. He was sure none of the Russians had ever visited the places themselves and obviously didn't know where they were. He wondered who had bought them and why. The drops were used twice in five years.

By 1969 Hugo had established himself as an authority on the Caribbean area by delivering at a Canadian economic conference in Winnipeg a well-received paper on the Cuban economy. Some of the information came from his trip to Cuba nine years earlier when he prepared a report for the Russians while serving in NATO. He had no scruples about duplicating the same report for both the East and the West; each side would frequently receive the same attention. In Peru and Haiti he would soon perform services pleasing to both the KGB and the Canadian International Development Agency.

In the spring of 1970 Herrmann visited Hugo again in the university cafeteria at Laval. Instructions had been received. Could the professor be in Vienna on the first Friday in June to rendezvous at the Hochstadtplatz? Someone would be waiting there to see him. The money for the journey was in a brown sealed envelope in the mailbox in his office.

Herrmann didn't have all the details but the Soviets were about to embark on a massive immigration program of Jews to Israel—perhaps three hundred thousand over several years. The Kremlin urgently needed information. Would a sudden influx of Jews, including many Russian liberals who were troublesome to Russia, disrupt Israeli life by placing an insufferable strain on the economy? What would it cost to set up a number of Russian immigrants in business in the Jewish state? Hugo would not admit this later, but the funds required to set up immigrants in business meant that selected KGB immigrants would be expected to spy for the Soviets. At the end of Hugo's visit to Israel the KGB wanted a report on the country's economy and the possibility of planting Soviet agents in the country. The Russians always expressed great satisfaction with Hugo's economic analyses, which were models of conciseness and relevant detail. Altogether the tasks should not take much more than a month.

Although the marriage to his Italian wife was coming to an end and would not last out the year, Hugo arranged for his wife Fiorella to spend the summer in Rome with their two-year-old son George William while the two older children remained with his mother in Ottawa. In May, as instructed, Hugo proceeded to Vienna, alone, to attend the meeting. Meanwhile, he had made it known at the university that he intended to do research on the Siege of Rhodes in 1480, a long-delayed project. This meant a side trip to Turkey where the historic canons that were used in the siege were on exhibit. The Order of St. John's of Jerusalem had conveniently commissioned the professor's study. Rhodes and Turkey were but a short flight from Israel, and a side journey to that country would not be noticed as anything out of the ordinary for a curious traveller like the professor, who was known for his extensive wanderings about Europe.

In Vienna Hugo met his old handler Paul at the coffee house near the Hochstadtplatz. It was like old times again. This was the first time the Canadian had seen the Russian in seven years. Paul confirmed everything that Herrmann had discussed in Quebec, and agreed that the research in Rhodes and Istanbul was an excellent cover. Hugo should visit the sites of his proposed research quickly and then allow himself plenty of time, at least a month, for his duties in Israel. Then in late July they would meet again back in Vienna for further talks. Paul issued a stern warning before they parted: beware of the Mossad, the Israeli secret service. The Jews had developed an intelligence service that was dangerous, unequalled and probably the most knowledgeable in the world about the Soviet Union. But as a Canadian professor, Hugo certainly would be treated well. Israel and Canada had good relations but little or no intelligence liaison. Then Paul gave his friend the addresses of two Russian agents in the Middle East: one lived in the old city of Jaffa while the other dwelt in a Beirut convent. The latter Hugo would never see, and it is doubtful that he saw the first.

Before Hugo went to Israel he dispatched several letters to announce he would be arriving that summer. Two of them were sent to the department of economics at the Hebrew University of Jerusalem where he would spend a week, off and on, studying in the library. Most certainly another communication went to the

Weitzman Institute in Rehovot. That letter was never answered, but Israelis are notoriously bad letter writers.

A statement made in a *Reader's Digest* article that the professor was sent to Israel to discover whether that country had the atomic bomb is, to say the least, farfetched. There is no evidence to support this view. The Mossad, however, would be curious about the activities of the visiting professor and more than a little interested in the background of the man himself.

From Hugo's own statements made later under interrogation, he claimed he went to Israel to prepare a report on the proposed infiltration of Soviet agents and how they could best be integrated into Israeli life. He prepared a ten-page memorandum, which was given to Paul in Vienna in July 1970. It revealed in great detail the method by which agents could take up positions unnoticed in Israeli society. Large-scale immigration to Israel began a few years later in 1974 and actually reached as many as fifty thousand a year for three years.

In addition to economic research at the Hebrew University, however, Hugo did visit Elat on the Red Sea, stopping off at Beersheba where atomic research was reputedly in progress. Israel has an extraordinarily tight security system surrounding all atomic research and a fiercely loyal staff. Breaches in security in sensitive areas of research in the country are practically unknown. The report he gave to Paul did, in fact, include a number of peripheral conclusions regarding the possession of an atomic device, although these were largely deduced guesses. Most Israelis, as well as the intelligence services of the Western world, know what is going on in that small country, and it was common knowledge that Israel had a small bomb of about four kilotons, roughly of Hiroshima size. But it would be tested against an enemy only under extreme provocation in wartime or as a last resort.

Several professors Hugo met at the Hebrew University invited him out for dinner at the King David Hotel, and the Canadian posed a few questions; he had a charming, self-effacing way of asking for information. He conveyed a sense of harmless innocence. It wasn't contrived. It was his natural manner and always brought results. As a consequence of Hugo's conversation at this dinner he obtained a certain amount of military intelligence that was largely gossip. Thus, a page of Hugo's report dealt with military equipment.

While Hugo did not supply any atomic information of any use, it is entirely possible that the information he relayed to Paul that July in Vienna formed a basis for some of the Soviets' major policy decisions on emigration of Russian Jewry. From references the Soviet agent made to Hugo in Vienna and in communications from Herrmann in 1972 in Quebec City, it is evident that the Israeli report was read by Politburo members. Thus Hugo was convinced that his favourable recommendations contained in the papers he sent to the KGB contributed substantially to the release of oppressed Russian Jewry. In the same document he established guidelines for a Soviet spy network that could operate in the Jewish state. As Hugo himself admitted, "there were covert undertones [in his instructions] for sending agents there."

At Hugo's departure from Lod Airport in July the immigration officer leafed slowly through the Canadian's passport, taking a little longer than normal. Then the official excused himself and quickly disappeared with the passport into a small cubicle where he checked a file of photographs. The first two pages of the Canadian's document were photocopied. It took no more than a minute.

"Was anything wrong?" Hugo asked the official when he returned.

"Absolutely nothing, Professor Hambleton. Canadian passports are sometimes stolen. It was simply a routine check. My apologies for the inconvenience."

Hugo was satisfied. He had no reason for suspicion. He enjoyed Israel, and he would come back, but now he would quickly proceed to complete his research on the ostensible object of his trip to Europe, the Siege of Rhodes. One of the professors at the dinner at the King David Hotel, however, had worked for Israeli intelligence. He had been wary of the questions the Canadian professor had asked. Why was a non-Jew so interested in the possible immigration to Israel of Soviet Jewry when so very few people even in Israel were aware this would take place? In 1970 the change of Soviet policy was known only to a handful of individuals in high places. Beginning that year, therefore, the Mossad quietly began to investigate the Canadian professor. When Hugo returned to Israel in 1975 with an Oriental woman companion who carried a radio receiver, the Mossad already had a thick file on him. They suspected he was a Soviet agent, and passed this information on to MI5, which took no action. Nor did MI5, as the Mossad assumed, transmit this intelligence to Canada. The Arabists in the British Foreign Office had muzzled all meaningful cooperation between the Mossad and British intelligence. Useful liaison between the two governments had virtually ceased, much to the detriment of England.

Before the professor returned to Vienna, he travelled to the island of Rhodes and then Istanbul to record on film the fortifications and canons that related to the siege. Dutifully, as promised, the Order of St. John's of Jerusalem would have a full account of the historic event.

– CHAPTER EIGHT –

The Americas

Hugo had become an accepted authority on the affairs of Latin America, and this position was further established at the meeting of the Canadian Association of Latin American Studies in 1971 in Mexico City when he was elected president. That same year the Canadian International Development Agency (CIDA) invited him to act as their advisor in their aid program to Peru. Laval University granted him a leave of absence for one year.

As the fortune of the Canadian professor prospered, the KGB hoped their own fortune would as well. His growing success as a respected scholar, a man of achievement in his chosen field, made him infinitely more attractive in Soviet eyes. And, as Hugo had learned, their eyes were everywhere. An important event had occurred in far-off Peru that had been overlooked and could be of considerable benefit to the Soviets. The Canadian would be given the opportunity to help shape the policy of a nonaligned American state in a way that would be favourable to his masters.

General Velasco Alvarado of Peru was a remarkable man by any standards. He was born to poverty but rose to the high rank of general in the army. In his youth at the military academy in Lima he studied Marxist theory, which was part of the standard curriculum of the school. Although he himself was not a Communist, upon coming to power as head of the military junta in 1968, Alvarado immediately established close relations with the Eastern bloc countries. He wanted to emulate the nonalignment policies of Tito's Yugoslavia. His government became known as Peru's "earthquake generation" of radical colonels. Alvarado was a phenomenon. The grinding misery of the majority of Peruvians was always on his mind. As the ruling member of the junta, Alvarado became known as "the people's general." He enacted bold, new land reforms and nationalized vast American holdings in the north of Peru—an act that made him unpopular in Washington. The peasants had suffered for generations, and he saw no solution to Peru's problem of poverty as long as his people were mercilessly exploited.

Into this environment came Professor Hambleton as part of the CIDA team.

While at Laval Hugo had applied for service in CIDA, which came under the responsibility of External Affairs. Therefore his posting to Peru had come about largely on his own initiative and with KGB approval. His recommendations would direct Canadian money into Peru, but more vital would be the Canadian's personal relationship with the easily approachable general. Within days the Canadian became the general's close advisor, ensconced in the Gobierno Palace, a large, baroque-style building of painted white stone protected by high, ornate iron gates. Hugo's suite on the second floor overlooked the Playa del Armas.

The situation was made to measure for the KGB, offering them unrivalled opportunity to have their man exert influence on a South American government that was bitterly anti-American. For the Communists, Hugo's position was ideal, and it wouldn't cost Russia a penny. Canada was paying the bill. Lima was an excellent observation post for the Soviets to overlook the world of South America, a continent buried in a depthless poverty and suffering from endemic corruption, and Peru was ripe for exploitation of its anti-American bias. Yet the United States was fumbling badly in its attempt to counter the grotesque anti-"Yanqui" image built up over half a century.

During the Canadian's six-month stay in Lima and immediately after, there was a noticeable increase in the political and economic activity between the Communist countries and the junta of Alvarado. And the Communist-dominated unions, in the vanguard of change, assumed a new and commanding position.

In the winter of 1971 Paul met the professor in Lima to discuss strategy relating to the job in Peru. Recommendations from an official of the Canadian government could carry weight unrelated to the relatively small investment Canada was making in the Peruvian economy. Alvarado respected Canada and admired its way of life.

The general became seriously ill in 1972, thus cutting short his opportunity to complete his radical economic and political reforms. One of these reforms was a drastic economic and political realignment away from the West and toward Eastern Europe. The enlightened military dictatorship of Alvarado

which began with such great promise gave way at last to a
conservative civilian government, and Hugo returned to his
professional duties at Laval in January 1972. The Canadians
and the Russians congratulated their man for his successful
mission. They were both well pleased with the results of his work
in South America.

1973 - 1975

Canada was so satisfied with the professor's mission on behalf of
CIDA to Peru that the government appointed him to head a
second project of agrarian reform for the Haitian dictatorship of
Paul Duvalier which would begin in 1973.

By this time Hugo's turbulent second marriage had ended.
Among other complaints, Fiorella accused her husband of
having various affairs, including an unpardonable liaison with
her sister while she was visiting in Quebec City. In a violent
argument one night in the St. Foy apartment, Hugo's hot-
blooded sister-in-law attacked him in a fit of anger, tearing off his
shirt, kicking, biting and screaming until she was subdued,
largely due to her own exhaustion. Shortly thereafter, Fiorella
moved out, and Hugo remained alone in the apartment with his
youngest son George William. It was with a sense of relief that he
accepted the Haiti assignment, and he planned to take his little
son with him. The boy was a quiet lad, introspective and bright
like Hugo. Because of the unsettled marital status of his parents,
he had developed an amazing sense of independence for a child
of five. The two older children now lived with their mother, and
sometimes their grandmother Bessie, in Ottawa. The remarkable Bessie was eighty-five years old, still brimming with
physical vigour and intellectual alertness. But she was having
trouble communicating as she grew progressively deaf, and this
caused her anger and annoyance. She would defy old age to the
last, but old age was having the last word.

Herrmann came to Quebec almost once a month, and it was
through him Hugo advised his KGB contacts that he would accept
CIDA's offer to head the program in Haiti. Meanwhile as a
prelude to his new job Hugo travelled to Mexico, Tobago and
Trinidad in June of that year to recruit teachers and make the
preliminary investigations in preparation for his new task. The
reports and the benefits of all his research went not only to the
Canadian government, which was financing the project, but also

to Herrmann, who transmitted the material to the KGB.

These reports, and subsequent ones relating to the Caribbean, were valuable political intelligence on the developing islands of the region, as valuable as those on South America. Subversion in the Caribbean had a high priority for the Soviets— but to engage in subversion, one had to have knowledge of the area, and Hugo gave them that. Keen analytical judgement was the quality the Soviets most admired in their man, and his detached, objective documents were required reading among high Soviet officials whose responsibility covered Latin America and the Caribbean. With the help of Cuban intelligence and now with their agent in Haiti, Soviet aims of subversion could be further advanced.

In the autumn of 1973 Herrmann contacted Hugo in Mexico City by a letter sent to a postal address used extensively by the KGB. His message read: "Your reports are appreciated. In your new position for the Canadian government you can perform a great service as a policy maker."

The implications were clear. The professor was to continue to steer the officials he met in the underdeveloped countries toward cooperation with Eastern Europe. But this was a risky business. The Canadian preferred only to supply information, which was far less compromising and also the type of work he enjoyed doing. In Peru under Velasco Alvarado his task had been easier. Alvarado had been a reformer, anti-American. But Haiti was a small, corrupt feudal state where change was deliberately stifled by the dictator Paul Duvalier. Nevertheless, Haiti was a good base from which to communicate with Cuba and those nearby impoverished islands whose deep political unrest made them ripe for subversion.

In September 1973 Hugo and his young son arrived in Haiti. They lived in a beautiful white concrete villa in the suburbs of Port-au-Prince, part of a small, protected compound of exclusive homes that belonged to friends and relatives of "Baby Doc," the ruling dictator. The brutal secret police called the Ton Ton Macoute beat and bullied the humble islanders into submission for the slightest infraction of the law. But Hugo enjoyed his comfortable sojourn in Haiti; he lived like a privileged prince, enjoying all the advantages of his position as head of the mission. At a call he could have one of several Haitian mistresses and numerous servants to take care of his wants.

His brief relationship with the twenty-two-year-old Haitian woman Maria Fleuries has already been mentioned. A daughter of one of Duvalier's cousins, she became the professor's travelling companion on a journey to Europe where he pretended she was a kind of hostage taken in exchange for the guaranteed welfare of his son, left with the Fleuries family in Port-au-Prince. The somewhat farfetched story was spread among his friends, but the truth was that the Haitian woman would conveniently detract attention from the real purpose of his journey, which was to attend to his KGB business in Europe. The promise of marriage Hugo had to make before he could obtain consent to take Maria with him created a number of complications from which he would eventually emerge unscathed.

In the winter of 1974 Herrmann came unannounced to Port-au-Prince. With Hugo's help he arranged for the government to supply a helicopter to fly over the island for the supposed purpose of producing a documentary on the country. Conveniently, Herrmann's visit served as a way to issue instructions on what policy should be followed in Haiti and what recommendations would be made to the Haitians through CIDA. The Soviets wanted intelligence that would enable them to make a more comprehensive assessment not only on Haiti but on all the Caribbean islands, especially those islands undergoing major political convulsions like Trinidad and Tobago. Herrmann stayed two nights in Port-au-Prince, and one of those nights overlapped my visit. Herrmann departed Haiti with a summary of Hugo's activities on the island as well as a number of memoranda prepared by other members of the Canadian team.

While Hugo was in Haiti, he was also visited at least once by the Cuban intelligence agent, Ricardo Escardin, whom he had met in Havana some years before. Together they formulated common objectives for the area and exchanged intelligence.

On December 22, 1974, Hugo left Port-au-Prince with Maria Fleuries for New York; from there they flew immediately to London, where they lodged at a second-class hotel off the Bayswater Road. The Haitian woman seldom left the premises, and when she ventured out, she felt so ill at ease she was anxious to return again to the security of her room. She had had enough of Europe and yearned for the parochial life of Port-au-Prince with the protection her family could give her.

Friends who observed Hugo during his London stay couldn't help detecting his listlessness and his anxiety. He was deeply troubled, but he kept his anxieties to himself. Perhaps it was a premonition that after twenty-six years in the service of the KGB, luck was slowly running out. Or perhaps the lives he led had grown too much to cope with, as had the loneliness of his existence. He had two broken marriages behind him. His children were growing up without a family life, deeply unsettled. The insidious belief that sooner or later most Soviet spies were caught must have occasionally seized him. He could share these feelings with no one. He lived lives that ran parallel, but the KGB life dominated all of them and like some vicious malignancy was slowly devouring the others. But there was no way back.

Herrmann was merely a conduit who transmitted instructions. Hugo didn't completely trust him, perhaps because he was too much like an American. He had adopted all their outward qualities and perhaps one day might develop all their beliefs. If Herrmann had not given Hugo indisputable proof of his identity, he would not have believed he was a Soviet officer. Indeed, the fear often crossed his mind that perhaps Herrmann worked for the CIA as a double agent. Hugo would never have been able to identify with Herrmann as he could with Paul. When asked years later: "Why are you protecting Paul? Are you still loyal to him?" the professor answered: "What's wrong with that?"

On his visit to London in 1975 Hugo kept an appointment in the British Museum with his Soviet contact. During this brief meeting, held in one of the study rooms off the main hall, plans were hatched for the Canadian's European travels.

Hugo left London with Maria for Torremolinos in early January. The Costa del Sol was unseasonably warm, tropically lush, that year, and he hoped a few days of rest would refresh him. But Maria was dull and uninteresting and was becoming a liability. After a week, having had all he could take of the Fleuries' daughter, he changed his mind about staying in Europe and flew back to Haiti on January 27, 1975. Depositing Maria thankfully with her family, Hugo explained to the parents that because of complications in his own divorce from his Italian wife, marriage with Maria was out of the question.

A few days later a phone call came from Herrmann that he should prepare his itinerary so that he would be in Vienna that spring. No reason was given. In six months Hugo's Haitian assignment would be over, and in spite of many distractions, it was coming to a successful conclusion.

In the spring of 1975 Hugo's passport displayed a bewildering array of stamps marking passages between Port-au-Prince, New York, Mexico, London, Paris, Torremolinos, Miami and then finally Montreal. At the hunting-lodge drop Hugo left a message giving the schedule for his forthcoming European trip, which was to be transmitted to the appropriate KGB authority. In the message, written on a one-time code pad, Hugo gave the exact time of his visit that spring to the Hochstadtplatz.

– CHAPTER NINE –

The
East

The professor looked forward to the rendezvous in Vienna where he expected to meet Paul. It would be a welcome diversion to his assignment in Haiti, which he disliked. The compelling personality of Paul had been branded upon Hugo for all time, and as long as his image was before him, Hugo felt safe. Without this man there would be a dreaded emptiness in his relationship with the KGB, and he would be forced to rely totally on himself. All the awesome might of the Soviet secret apparatus was symbolized by Paul. But Hugo proved to be stronger than he believed possible during his personal trials that still lay ahead.

He remained in Vienna for three days, and each day at the appointed hour and location near the Hochstadtplatz he waited in vain for Paul to appear. No chalk marks criss-crossed on the wall leading to the coffee house appeared to indicate a meeting would take place. Hugo didn't doubt for a moment that the Russian was delayed because of some urgent matter. Perhaps he had been called away suddenly to a trouble spot somewhere. Then again, Paul might be under surveillance as Hugo himself could be. Somehow he didn't think so. Although the circumstances were strange, the Canadian was sure that there was some simple explanation.

On the fourth day Hugo reluctantly decided to leave the city and continue on to Israel, where he wanted to spend several weeks visiting friends at the Hebrew University. Before he left Vienna he mailed a letter to the East Berlin contact address outlining his plans. He would return to keep a new appointment at a date in late August and hoped Paul would be at the Hochstadtplatz to greet him at that time.

Hugo left Vienna in the company of an Oriental girlfriend who had accompanied him from Paris. From Vienna they travelled by train to Athens. The missed meeting with Paul bothered him, and he double-checked the date in his diary to make sure he had not made a mistake. He had not. The Canadian led a carefully ordered and structured existence, and no matter which life he was leading, all his activities were minutely chronicled. Every item, each task, was conscientiously entered in a notebook. He hoped nothing serious had happened to Paul who in his own mind was indestructible.

On July 8, Hugo and his companion flew from Athens into Lod Airport. The Oriental girl carried Hugo's shortwave receiver through customs. No questions were asked, but the Mossad was alerted to the arrival. In the lounge, he rejoined the girl, who had passed through the formalities ahead of him, then the two took a taxi from the airport to their hotel on Hayarkon Street in Tel Aviv.

Over a hundred and sixty thousand Soviet Jews had come to Israel since 1971. The Mossad was quite aware of Soviet intentions to plant "illegals" as agents, many of whom used Israel as a stopover for a year or two before going on to Canada or the United States. The Israelis had taken measures to weed out the spies and had enlarged their a file on Professor Hambleton. The question one asks is, If the Mossad suspected in the early 1970s that the Canadian was a KGB agent, why did the RCMP only become interested in his activities in 1977 and then only through the accidental arrest of a Soviet agent in New York City?

Hugo spent three weeks in Israel, and during that time he was constantly under surveillance by the Israeli secret service. Perhaps he knew he was under observation, since he did nothing to arouse suspicion. He spent a good deal of time working at the library of the Hebrew University in Jerusalem or talking to academic acquaintances or travelling with his girlfriend by bus from one town to another. One night when Hugo returned to the room where he lodged in Jerusalem, he inspected the back of his Grundig shortwave set, as was his habit. Immediately he became alarmed. One of the screws in the backing plate was loose. He checked the other screws and found that several more had been tampered with. Someone had hastily inspected his equipment.

Outwardly the professor always remained calm. He never lost his composure or displayed a great deal of emotion, even when he was frightened and under considerable pressure. His feelings registered distantly and were weighed in relative terms, almost clinically. He would not be imprisoned in Israel, he knew that. There would be suspicion perhaps, but no real evidence that he had done anything except acquire information through open sources. His KGB reports in Israel were always written outside the country, and his copious notes were not meaningful to anyone but himself. The Israelis would be unable to connect him with the Soviet espionage system. At least Israel was a democratic nation with traditions of justice that its people guarded jealously. In the Arab gulf there would be no safeguards against espionage, and he hoped to travel to Jiddah soon. Fortunately there was no communication between the Arabs and the Jews, so he had little to fear that the Mossad would communicate its suspicions to other Middle East countries.

Hugo checked the frequency on the radio dial. It, too, had been altered. Once or twice he had tried to pick up, unsuccessfully, the old Moscow frequency, although he always moved the dial to a new position when he switched off the set. Hugo said nothing to his Oriental companion, but he asked the concierge of the pension whether anyone had asked for him. She replied in the negative.

The incident convinced Hugo that he was no longer a welcome guest in the country and undoubtedly expedited his departure. He decided to return to Vienna; but since his departure from Israel would be sooner than anticipated, he mailed another letter to the contact address in East Berlin to notify Paul of his new date of arrival. He took the precaution of sending it from the central post office without any signature or any return address. He fervently hoped Paul would receive it and be at the Vienna rendezvous.

On August 2, Hugo departed from Lod Airport without any difficulty. He went on alone to Athens while his girlfriend returned to Paris. The professor had serious business with Paul and didn't wish to be encumbered by the presence of a woman. He wanted to tell the KGB officer of the incident with the Mossad in Jerusalem, hoping that Paul would with a word or two calm all Hugo's fears and put them into perspective. He always did.

In Athens Hugo transferred to a train that would go to Vienna by way of Belgrade. He had almost a week before the proposed appointment with Paul. Train travel was much cheaper than plane and gave Hugo the leisure to write and catch up on his reading. He found the train more relaxing, more peaceful, than the frantic rush through the airports. Sitting in the same compartment with him was the Galeva family from Belgrade. They said they were returning home from a holiday in Macedonia. The daughter, Lili, was a twenty-two-year-old student of English and science at the University of Belgrade. She

spoke reasonable English, and Hugo and Lili struck up an amicable conversation during most of the trip.

He told her he was a visiting professor from Canada doing research throughout the summer on economic subjects in the Middle East. He hoped to stay a few days in Belgrade en route to Vienna. Hugo had not really intended to stay in Belgrade, but the meeting with the girl had changed his mind.

"One day I would like to travel to Canada and the United States," Lili had said before they arrived in the Belgrade station.

Hugo had already envisioned a task for Lili. She would make an ideal travelling companion—like his other girls—but beyond that, as a Yugoslav she might be put to good use. She could in time have a role as a courier.

Lili was not very tall, about five feet three inches, with thick black hair, high cheekbones, and tear-shaped eyes. A slight girl of plain appearance, she would be noticed only for her distinctly Slavic features. Lili's father worked as a photographer for the state-owned motion picture studio in Belgrade. Neither he nor his wife spoke English but were very impressed that a person of Hugo's position would be interested in their daughter. On the afternoon of his arrival in Belgrade Hugo checked into the Slavija Hotel.

Shortly after, the Canadian took a taxi to the room where Lili lived alone near the university. He spent the remainder of the afternoon and a good part of the evening with his new Yugoslavian friend and found her immediately receptive to his advances. They agreed to correspond regularly when Hugo returned to Quebec. The next spring he promised to make the necessary arrangements for her to visit him as his guest in Canada.

At the end of the day when Hugo returned to the Slavija Hotel, two sombre-looking men were waiting for him in the lobby. He didn't need to be told who the strangers were and what they wanted. Their close-cropped hair, their ill-fitting suits and the stiff formality of their approach indicated the nature of their work. The taller and bulkier of the two secret policemen spoke English.

"Professor Hambleton?" he enquired.

"Yes." Hugo, calm and quiet, waited. He had no contacts in Yugoslavia nor had he been requested to perform any mission there for the KGB. The Yugoslavs identified themselves as members of the police. However, they belonged to the KOS, the Yugoslavian counter-intelligence. A car was parked outside, and Hugo swiftly and without explanation was conducted to their headquarters, fingerprinted and subjected to a close interrogation as to the purpose of his journey to Belgrade. The Canadian claimed he was there as a tourist. The questions asked by the Yugoslavs ranged over a long list of subjects, including Hugo's work at NATO, but the interrogators concentrated mainly on the names of certain people in the country, all of whom were unknown to him. Eventually, he was shown a series of photographs and asked whether he recognized any of the men. Several were KGB agents, at least one of whom Hugo had met in Vienna, but he said he recognized none of them. The interrogator was cold but courteous. At one point the professor threatened to call the Canadian ambassador whom he said he knew personally— but this had little effect. Lili's name was never brought into the discussion, although the police undoubtedly knew of his visit to her room earlier that day.

The interrogators had taken possession of his tickets and passport and knew of his travel itinerary. They wanted to know why Hugo had gone to Israel, the reason for his trip to Vienna, and why he had stopped in Belgrade. He was a tourist sight-seeing for a day, he said. The large Yugoslav who spoke English and was in charge of the investigation handed back the personal documents late that night with the pronouncement: "We will escort you to the railroad station. There is a late train to Austria. You have been ordered to leave Yugoslavia immediately."

Hugo was driven to his room at the Slavija Hotel and was watched while he packed his bags. He was then taken to the station and, still shaken by the ordeal, put on board the Vienna train. No effort was made at any time during this episode to contact the Canadian embassy. At this point the Yugoslavs knew of Hugo's KGB connection, so did the Israelis and possibly the Americans, but the Canadians remained in blissful ignorance.

The grilling in Belgrade could have been American- or Israeli-inspired, a deliberate effort to investigate the Canadian in cooperation with the Yugoslavs, who had been informed by the Mossad of Hugo's movements before he could reach his KGB rendezvous in Vienna. One of the main topics in Hugo's interrogation by the Yugoslav secret police was Israel. Perhaps they were doing for the Mossad what the Israelis did not wish to do themselves.

1975 – 1977

In Vienna Hugo was visibly relieved when he arrived at the

rendezvous in the Hochstadtplatz. Paul was waiting for him.

Instead of entering the café where they usually met, the two men went for a walk along the banks of the Danube, and Hugo told the KGB officer of his interrogation in Belgrade. Hugo did not bother to mention his liaison with Lili. Paul made it clear the KGB had very little to do with the Yugoslav security service. Relations were not too good with Yugoslavia in view of the considerable military assistance Yugoslavia received from the United States. It was more than likely that the questioning was inspired by the CIA or the Israelis. The Canadian's interrogation was disturbing news to the KGB officer but did not necessarily mean their man was in any imminent danger. There could be numerous reasons for his detention which concerned Hugo's Middle East journeys. Nevertheless, Paul was convinced that the Mossad was connected with the Belgrade incident and did not then believe the interrogation related to either his European or North American activities.

Then the Russian switched to a more immediate subject. He said he was now acting on instructions from the highest authority. Plans were already made for Hugo to leave that same day for Moscow where important discussions were scheduled. Paul didn't elaborate on the nature of the discussions but simply presented the subject in his normal matter-of-fact manner which indicated that irrevocable decisions had already been reached. The Russian knew that if he told Hugo he was ordered to Moscow on the highest authority, the Canadian would not argue.

The Canadian was instructed to immediately pack his bags and be in front of the Vienna railroad station in two hours. A car would arrive there, and the driver would ask a slight variation of the familiar question, "Do you have any etchings for sale?" Hugo's reply would be, "Yes, I do, but in Paris. Not here." He would then enter the limousine and be taken across the Austrian frontier into Czechoslovakia. The black limousine would be recognizable by its diplomatic licence plates. Paul then departed, leaving Hugo standing alone on the pavement. Recovering from the effect of the unexpected news of his immediate visit to Russia, he hailed a taxi and went back to his hotel.

Hugo did exactly as he was told. He packed his bags, went to the railroad station and waited. At the appointed time a black limousine drew up to the curb and stopped before him. The driver opened the window and asked the appropriate question and received the correct reply. The back door of the car opened, and Hugo entered, joining a Russian diplomat who sat stiffly in the backseat. The vehicle drove off. In the car Hugo's passport was taken away, and he was issued a new travel document written in Russian with his photograph affixed. He could not read the Cyrillic writing but assumed the document gave him diplomatic status.

The Canadian was told to remain silent at the Austrian check-point. The border guard quickly waved through the diplomatic entourage, and the car sped off in the direction of the Bratislava Airport, about an hour's drive away. At the airport Hugo and his Russian escort boarded the waiting Russian aircraft. The turbo-prop plane was filled with Soviet military personnel and a number of civilians. After a stopover in Warsaw the aircraft flew directly on to a military base near Moscow.

No one had adequately prepared Hugo for the sudden and surprising Moscow journey. He was still nervous from his Belgrade experience. The Yugoslavian police had been hostile, subjecting the Canadian to an unrelenting, polite but aggressive barrage of questions. They had made it clear to him that, although they could not prevent him from returning to Yugoslavia if he chose, he would do so at his own risk. Despite this warning, Lili Galeva still enticed him, and he wanted to see her again.

Hugo had no passport, no means of identification, and no one but the Russians were aware of his entry into the Soviet Union. He was, he realized then, a person who could vanish from the face of the earth without a trace. The fear that the KGB had discovered some evidence to cast suspicion on his reliability increased his tension. But Hugo reassured himself there could be no logical reason for the KGB to doubt his loyalty.

At the Moscow military airfield where the turbo-prop plane landed, he was warmly greeted by Paul and a young blond-haired Russian who would act as the Canadian's personal escort for the next six days in Russia. The blond man spoke American-style English fluently and conducted his guest to a waiting limousine driven by a chauffeur. There were no immigration formalities to pass through and within minutes the car was on the road speeding into Moscow.

Shortly after the limousine entered the city, Hugo's companion proudly pointed out the ornate palace of the KGB headquarters on Dzherhinsky Square, with the grim, grey structure of Lubyanka prison looming behind. About ten minutes later the car crossed Red Square and skirted the Kremlin, stopping several blocks further in front of a large apartment building on Gorky Street. Hugo's suite of ornately furnished rooms was on the third floor. A large, attractive dining room, two bedrooms, and a kitchen with a well-stocked larder of food and liquor made up the apartment. This would be the Canadian's home for the duration of his visit.

The Moscow mission was a serious working session of seminars, and not, as Hugo was to describe later, a tourist journey. Appointments were scheduled with Kremlin officials of a superior rank who were responsible for the policies affecting the nations of South America and the Caribbean. The conversations took place over luncheons and dinners lavishly served by a waiter at the apartment, with plenty of Vodka, caviar and other delicacies. There were no interpreters present.

> All the people who came to see me spoke English more or less fluently. This surprised me. But it made the meetings easy, friendly. The company was good. I gave my analysis of the political and economic conditions in Chile. I was listened to respectfully. They didn't expect me to change the world. They were not malicious people. They were very curious people and thought, incorrectly, that I had some great gems of wisdom to give. I think they had an inflated idea of my importance because of my work for the Canadian International Development Agency, my advisory capacity to the government of Peru. I might have helped to straighten out some misconceptions about Western policy. They were hostile toward the governments of Chile and Haiti. They listened to me because they believed I wasn't hostile.

The professor also discussed agrarian reform in Russia. He was pleasantly surprised to learn that the Russian attitude favoured a type of individual ownership as opposed to the old idea of collectivism.

The dinner meetings were interspersed with sightseeing journeys in the company of Paul and the escort, with one memorable excursion to the Leningrad Museum—full, as Hugo remarked jokingly, "of bourgeois, capitalist, Impressionist paintings." By an amazing coincidence, one of the West's great capitalists and a native of Russia, Armand Hammer, had just completed arrangements to take the Leningrad's Impressionist paintings on a world tour. He was in Moscow at the same time.

On the fourth day of Hugo's visit, Paul gave notice that at dinner that evening there would be a special guest, and Hugo should feel honoured. When asked who it would be, Paul only smiled secretively and said the man would be introduced to him on arrival. In the event he should not come it was better not to mention his name; that way, no one would be disappointed. At eight o'clock that evening all the assembled guests were present except for those who would occupy the three vacant chairs. The table was lavishly set with fine linen and silver and sparkling crystal. Two vases of flowers were at either end of the table. An unopened bottle of vintage champagne was cooling in a silver bucket. Whoever was coming to dinner that night warranted very special attention. Paul and his blond friend were present, as well as two guests introduced to Hugo as an assistant and a chief director of the First Foreign Directorate of the KGB. If these men held such august positions, Hugo wondered with growing excitement for whom the three empty places were reserved. In the dinners that were held in the apartment the Canadian had noticed an order of protocol that was never violated. Lower officials invariably arrived first, followed by their superiors.

At a quarter past eight that evening there was a knock at the door and the blond-haired man jumped swiftly to his feet to answer. All the other guests rose. Into the room came a short, stocky energetic man wearing a pair of steel-rimmed spectacles. His manner was so reticent, so retiring, that Hugo waited for someone else to appear as the important guest. Two larger individuals escorted the smaller man to his place—obviously KGB bodyguards, whose eyes closely surveyed the other occupants of the room. Apparently satisfied, one of the escorts then shut the door. The blond man introduced the guest with considerable respect.

"This is Comrade Yuri Alexovich Andropov," he said.

Hugo stiffened at the name, but the KGB chief immediately put the Canadian at ease. He spoke English fluently. When they sat down to dinner the professor was seated next to Andropov, who removed his spectacles. This gave his face a kindly, benevolent expression. His voice was soft, his movements gentle, but his questions were forthright. During dinner he solicited Hugo's opinions and preferred to listen rather than talk.

Andropov's topics of conversation revolved around three main subjects for the two hours he spent at the apartment. The issue of anti-Semitism in America aroused his interest, and he asked Hugo whether that would become a serious problem in the future. The Canadian said he didn't think it would. Andropov was under the impression that the hundreds of thousands of Jews Russia allowed out were going to America, and Russia did not like the idea of losing that many talented people to its ideological enemy. The other major topics about which he sought knowledge were the Common Market and NATO. In Andropov's remarks that evening at dinner an attitude of appreciation subtly insinuated itself into the discussion, as if he had knowledge of Hugo's work on behalf of the KGB during his NATO days.

Whenever Andropov spoke, everyone listened, nodded, agreed and waited. Andropov, Hugo and Paul were the people whose conversation dominated the gathering. Before the KGB chief rose to leave with his escorts he made a proposal in the form of an offer to his foreign guest: "In America more than anywhere else we require people who can influence opinion. People like yourself, Professor Hambleton. In the Western electoral process a man of your accomplishment can obtain high political office. The financing of your political career would present no great problems for us."

Hugo nodded agreeably. It was a thought that had crossed his mind before. In the winter of that year when he returned to teach at Laval, the professor accepted an invitation to join one of the major Canadian political parties, but the person who made the suggestion, wisely in retrospect, never followed up on the offer.

The day before Hugo left Moscow he was visited by a woman called Natasha who was an expert on codes and secret means of communication. Like most of his visitors she spoke excellent English and mentioned in the course of the conversation that in the early sixties she had spent two years at a university in New England when her father was part of a Soviet delegation to the United Nations. She showed Hugo how to use secret inks, new one-time pads, and to expect secret messages by ordinary mail written on the inside of a normal airmail envelope. By treating the inside of the envelope with certain chemicals after it was slit open, messages, often accompanied by diagrams, would be revealed. Then came the instructions on the new *lumière* device or light, as it was sometimes known. A small metal box with a window display lit up into a series of numbers when tuned into Moscow reception. Music and sounds were translated into numerical groups, each number representing a letter of the alphabet. The groups, when translated into numbers, would yield the message.

Much was made of this light machine, but its usefulness was highly exaggerated. And because of the complexity of its construction it frequently failed to work. The "light" attached to a Grundig shortwave receiver would transmit instructions to Hugo. Since this "light" equipment was in short supply, it would be sent to Canada sometime within the year.

During the course of the four-hour instruction Natasha

brought up the name of Colonel Oleg Penkovsky. This might have been a warning. Penkovsky had been exposed, Natasha warned, because he was careless in the use of his equipment. It was an odd reference to make to the Canadian, but every Russian agent who defected to the West represented a personal danger to Hugo. In 1961 Penkovsky had offered his services as a double agent in Moscow to the CIA and the Canadians, both of whom rejected him as being too high a risk. The British thought differently and accepted him as a *bona fide*, high-level KGB official. Penkovsky handed over volumes of GRU and KGB documents and top-classified information to MI5 and the Americans.

He was later arrested along with a British businessman spy, James Greville Wynne, who was caught in Hungary in 1961. Greville Wynne was exchanged nine months later for a Soviet agent languishing in an English prison. According to the Russians, Penkovsky was shot. Some Western intelligence sources believe the Russian colonel was planted in the West to perform a disinformation service. In retrospect most of his spectacular disclosures, including Cuban missile intelligence, furthered Soviet aims.

The year 1975 was a kind of watershed in Hugo's life. He had received the supreme accolade that could be granted a Western agent: he had met the head of the KGB. This was a signal that the professor's role was being viewed more as a moulder of opinions than anything else. The Russians were convinced their man would progressively assume more influential positions on the councils of international bodies.

But Hugo's personality was undergoing deep-seated changes. The danger signs had been present for some time. The intricately woven tales to his friends were more than cover stories. The imagery bordered on the fantastic. And this fragmenting of his personality would increase as time went on. The flashing beacons that had been Hugo's points of reference in the dark life he led were receding, growing fainter. Paul, who had represented the greatest strength and influence, was over sixty. He spoke more often of his wife and family in Moscow, and his retirement could not be far off. Bessie was aged, deaf, with a fading memory, and Hugo could no longer count on her for advice. The spy was a lonely man. He could confide in no one. The excitement was turning slowly into fear and desolation. Moscow and its immense loneliness and impersonal atmosphere only intensified his anxiety. At the end of six days Hugo was glad to leave and return to Vienna.

From there Hugo wrote to Lili in Belgrade. She was still very much on his mind, and he reminded her by letter of her promise to correspond with him regularly at his Quebec City address. He travelled home by way of Paris and London where he kept his habitual rendezvous at the British Museum on a Friday afternoon. When he left Vienna he felt a strong desire to go directly to Belgrade, but the unpleasant memory of his recent interrogation deterred him. There would be other means of seeing Lili soon again.

By the time Hugo returned to Quebec, which was not until late August, a letter awaited from Lili at his apartment in St. Foy. He immediately wrote back suggesting that she come to Canada with her brother who would be leaving Belgrade the following spring to take employment in the United States for the summer.

The 1975-1976 academic year at Laval University was not uneventful. The Moscow visit left a deep, lasting impression upon Hugo. He had been pleased with the flattery and by the most favoured treatment received. Everyone in Moscow had been gracious, and the conversations had not turned to distasteful or contentious subjects. But beneath all the politeness and attention there had been an ominous and threatening quality that made Hugo aware that, for better or worse, his life was joined to the KGB forever.

- CHAPTER TEN -

The Final
Hours

Hugo had not had a visit from Herrmann for over six months, but he attributed no special significance to this. After all, Herrmann had responsibility for KGB operations throughout America, and his cover as a motion picture producer meant that he could be engaged in a project almost anywhere. Sooner or later Herrmann would show up. He always did.

In the autumn of 1975, in late September, the professor received a letter postmarked East Berlin. Inside the envelope was a blank sheet of paper which he threw away. He slit open the envelope, flattened it with the opened flap out on the table, and treated it with the chemical compound he had brought back from Moscow. Written instructions showed up in brown ink. Hugo was to go to the hunting lodge near Montreal where a document was hidden under a log wrapped in brown paper.

When he picked up the message at the lodge, it turned out to be a two-page document that did not make exciting reading. It contained new instructions to follow. On his next sabbatical he should make an effort to find employment at a university in Washington or New York State. The purpose was to befriend professors and other intellectuals who were members of economic think-tanks, particularly the Hudson Institute in New York, where many foreign policies were developed for the U.S. government. If all that failed, then his attention should turn in the direction of the Canadian External Affairs Department. Through External Affairs he could become associated with the opinion-makers of America. None of the suggestions appealed very much. In fact, Hugo believed they were absurd, and could see no logic in pursuing them. He was much more interested in developing his relations with Lili, with whom he was now exchanging warm and impassioned correspondence. She had accepted an invitation to come in late April of 1976 to Quebec City, and the professor had planned his spring and summer schedule to accommodate his newest girlfriend.

A second letter arrived from East Berlin before Christmas. The message contained inside the slit envelope gave the date, time and place of the arrival of the new light decoder that could translate the Moscow sounds into numerals. The decoder would be handed over to Hugo personally in the Place Ville Marie underground garage in downtown Montreal in February. An hour was chosen when the garage would be busy at the end of a normal working day and the transfer unlikely to be noticed. Hugo was instructed to park his own car in the garage at one of the numbered bays and wait for the delivery. Someone would make himself known.

Hugo followed these orders. He arrived at the Place Ville Marie on a cold mid-February day, making the journey from Quebec City. Well in advance of the hour, Hugo spent thirty minutes browsing through a bookstore in the upper shopping plaza before taking the escalator down to the garage. A small black Honda with a Quebec licence plate was stationed at the bay adjoining his own car. When Hugo approached the vehicle, a man behind the wheel of the Honda identified himself, immediately referring to the professor by name. The Honda owner, a middle-aged man who spoke in a fluent local French and whom Hugo had never seen before, went around to the trunk of his car, opened it and handed over a black plastic box about a foot long.

Hugo drove back to Quebec City, and as soon as he arrived home he opened the black box. A greyish metal machine about the size of a pound box of chocolates was inside. It could sit comfortably and unobtrusively on top of the Grundig shortwave set. No one would pay much attention to it. The professor could tell any inquisitive person the "light" was some kind of attachment or converter. With the Moscow radio schedule in his possession he was now ready to receive Moscow directly.

As the professor would mention later, the new spy paraphernalia added a stimulating new dimension to his life. "I was fascinated to see my code printing out, knowing someone in Moscow would be sending at the same time." But he would have much less use for the decoder than he anticipated. Indeed, it might have been a bit of a disappointment. He received infrequent transmissions, and often they were of no consequence. However, the following spring, before Lili arrived from Belgrade, the decoder lit up on schedule and ranged through its litany of numbers. It was a brief transmission. The message read: Happy Birthday. It was May 4, 1976. Hugo was fifty-four years old. The KGB had not forgotten.

That summer Hugo met with Lili as planned in Quebec City. From here they travelled through parts of New England, followed by a romantic journey south to Mexico. As a present to Lili, Hugo made arrangements for regular monthly payments of one hundred dollars to be transferred to her account in Belgrade in the Ljubljanska Banka. In between the monthly payments other amounts of two and three hundred dollars were sent to Lili.

The love affair was not all romance, however. Lili delivered messages for Hugo to Vienna on two trips between 1977 and 1978. It is almost certain that the Yugoslav secret police intercepted these messages and passed them on to Western sources. The chance encounter with Lili on the train to Belgrade as described by Hugo is also certainly only part of the truth. He sought out female travelling companions who provided excellent cover and fulfilled his own craving for female attention. It was a sign of his emotional immaturity that he chose women who he believed were young innocents and whom he could easily influence to serve him.

But Lili was tougher than she looked. She came from hardy Macedonian stock. She enjoyed the good times Hugo offered, and the money augmented her own meagre income. But she paid dearly for her gifts in the long interrogation that lasted for several weeks in November of 1979 in Belgrade at the hands of the Yugoslavian secret police, who wanted all the information she could give them about the Canadian.

Later she received international coverage in an article published in a widely distributed popular magazine. In one or more of the interviews held with the author of that article in Quebec City, Hugo allowed his imagination to roam freely on all subjects. Lili lay dying of terminal cancer, he said. The invention about Lili was only part of his imaginings. Later he repeated the Galeva story to the RCMP interrogators to throw them off the scent. His protection of Lili represented partially a kind of gallantry toward a woman with whom he had enjoyed a sporadic affair, but also he did not want her to be interrogated. She knew too much about his activities.

When he said that six thousand dollars, admittedly received from the KGB, would be used for her hospital treatment abroad, the story was all fiction. In 1983 Lili, in robust health, outsprinted Tim Miles, the *London Daily News* correspondent, down a Belgrade street and then outraced him up four flights of steep stairs in her apartment building. Miles, out of breath, finally pushed some questions on a piece of paper under the door. But Lili was too frightened to talk. He real fear was not for her health but for her safety, which had been jeopardized by her association with the professor. The Yugoslavs are very sensitive to KGB infiltration.

Fate was unkind to Rudi Herrmann. If it had not been, perhaps the Canadian would never have been caught in spite of his fears and strange premonitions of surveillance, and Herrmann's role would have been unchanged. But an incident on the streets of New York in 1977 altered all that.

Although the Yugoslavs and the Mossad were aware of Hugo's KGB connection, these intelligence services apparently kept the information to themselves, perhaps until they learned more about the nature of the Canadian's activities. This would be particularly true of the Mossad, which undoubtedly hoped the professor would return to Israel and be trapped in actual liaison with a Russian agent in that country. The Yugoslavs would be much less fussy about the due process of the law than the Israelis. But in the murky, deceitful world in which the spy dwells, nothing can be certain, including the motives of the Western democracies. No one in Canada knew about the professor, and if the Americans possessed prior knowledge about him, they kept the information closely guarded until Rudi Herrmann stumbled into the lap of the FBI.

He was driving slowly along a street on the west side of New York on a mission one cold winter day in 1977. He opened the window of his car and suddenly dropped an eight-inch length of lead pipe onto the curb in front of a fire hydrant. Without warning an unmarked car overtook Herrmann and ordered him to pull over. Inside the vehicle were two New York plainclothes policemen who by the merest chance were driving along the same street about fifty feet behind the KGB colonel. One more block and the police officers would have turned off into another road.

One of the detectives stepped out of his car and curiously but cautiously picked up the length of pipe, thinking it might be some kind of bomb. But inside was a rolled-up message in code addressed to another KGB agent. The detectives took Herrmann to the local police station and immediately phoned the FBI. After two days of intense questioning, Herrmann confessed to his true identity. It was a major coup for the Americans, and it had some far-reaching consequences. In exchange for immunity and the promise of a new life for himself, his wife and two children, Herrmann cooperated fully with the FBI. One of the first disclosures he made was about the presence of a trusted and important KGB agent in Canada: Professor Hugh George Hambleton. The FBI waited almost six months before they told their secret to the RCMP.

1978 - 1979

On a sunny May morning in 1978 three RCMP officers flew from Montreal to Logan Airport situated between the cities of Baltimore and Washington. They were greeted by two CIA agents and driven by a roundabout route toward an undisclosed destination. One of the RCMP officers was Inspector Frank Pratt, another was Sergeant Robert McIlroy. The third held a higher rank and was in charge of the RCMP party. In his pocket the third man carried a prepared list of thirteen questions. The CIA escorts drove their RCMP visitors over back country roads, doubling back on their tracks until the Canadians lost all sense of direction. They arrived at last at a large country home overlooking a lake in Maryland. Inside the house the RCMP officers were introduced to Colonel Rudolph Herrmann, late of the KGB.

The RCMP spent three hours with Herrmann asking their questions, which had to be approved by the CIA lawyers who sat in on the interrogation. The meeting was very friendly and cooperative. Herrmann and his disclosures that incriminated the Laval professor were recorded at length on video tape. When the questioning was over, the former KGB colonel with his CIA escorts and the RCMP contingent went out together for a friendly lunch.

When the RCMP finally prepared the operational plan to be directed against the Laval professor, they discovered that their man had already left for a sabbatical year in Europe. The security officials kept their closely guarded secret to themselves, put the video tape in a safe at their headquarters in Montreal, and waited patiently for him to return to Canada. Meanwhile they began to investigate the life of Hugh George Hambleton in depth.

The Canadian security service had no wish to put out an alarm for the arrest of the professor. So far, all they had was the word of a confessed KGB colonel that H.G. Hambleton had engaged in a kind of reportorial espionage. They had no proof of any indictable offence that he had committed. They were convinced he was working for the Russians, but they needed some hard evidence and for that they had to question the man himself.

It may have been that the leave of absence from Laval was no coincidence. The long silence of Herrmann, with whom he never felt very comfortable, had left the professor uneasy. Hugo asked to see Paul in the autumn after he completed some personal business in London and finished a paper on the petro-chemical industry relating to the Arab gulf states. One message came through on the decoder before he departed for Europe confirming the need for the rendezvous in Vienna at the end of the summer. If it was bad news, Hugo was in no hurry to hear about it.

In the early summer of 1978 the Canadian arrived in England carrying the Grundig radio and decoder. As mentioned earlier, he took up temporary residence at 357 Ben Jonson House in my apartment at the Barbican in London. I planned to be out of town during most of the sojourn, and he would have the place to himself. The availability of the Barbican was fortuitous for Hugo because this huge block of flats, constructed like the Bastille with mazes of passages and rabbit-warren dwellings, offered a kind of anonymity. But the British secret service knew the address.

Hugo intended to spend most of his days in London working in his quiet retreat at the British Museum on the petro-chemical paper. In the museum he would meet his contact at the regular table and at the appointed time once a week. To this day his British connection remains unknown; he has always adamantly refused to divulge the name of the person he saw inside the building.

At the end of each day Hugo would return to the Barbican. Now and then he would indulge in short journeys to the south coast of England and spend time in the small harbours and yacht marinas. He had of late developed an interest in sailing and joined a yacht club. Although he had practically no sailing experience, he was anxious to learn all he could about small craft.

As Hugo grew older, some of the glamour of his spying career had begun to wear off. Study and his academic pursuits were assuming a greater importance than his work for the KGB which was having a serious and destructive effect on his character. Perhaps if there was still a way out, he might have taken it, but none existed. Hugo loved the minute discoveries that came from painstaking research, the abstruseness, the isolation, the exclusivity of scholarship. The KGB also recognized this. Many of his assignments demanded scholarship first and spying second. In a way Hugo felt the tasks were related. Spying in its most esoteric sense was a kind of modern scholarship, he liked to believe. It frequently meant the joining together of diverse secret elements from the past and present and predicting the future. Long ago he had ceased to discuss with himself the moral dilemma that the problem once posed. He had the unusual ability to separate his worlds and to continue to function. Or so he thought.

Hugo wanted to remain in London until the middle of September and then slowly make his way through Paris and Vienna to Saudi Arabia. Through messages sent on his decoder Moscow had stressed on two occasions during the month the urgency of a Vienna meeting. But Hugo was taking his time. He had learned from past experience that many of the Russian requests for meetings were unimportant. Hugo was treating Paul's insistence on an immediate rendezvous in Vienna somewhat casually. He was anxious to finish his preliminary research on the gulf states in London before departing. Also, he hoped to fit in a journey to Belgrade to visit Lili before he saw Paul.

The leisurely atmosphere of the British Museum had enveloped him completely. There he felt secure without any sense of urgency or danger. And when he worked and studied he was liberated from all despair. Herrmann and his other Russian friends were suddenly remote, distant. He had no idea of the feverish activity in the RCMP security services that was now directed at himself, nor of the fact that INTERPOL had been alerted and the British security service had been asked to keep a watch on the Canadian while in England. But it would be difficult to follow his movements on the Continent. None of the European countries were interested in Professor Hambleton.

The RCMP were fearful that their man might disappear forever, might defect, even though all indications at Laval and with his mother in Ottawa suggested that Hugo would be returning to Canada after his sabbatical. But no one knew exactly when; nor were they certain of his movements. The RCMP waited patiently. Sooner or later they expected to get their man.

An emergency order received on the radio while in London impressed upon him the need to proceed to Vienna. Hugo finally wrote to the East Berlin address giving the time of his proposed arrival. Reluctantly he left England, stopping first in Paris, then Amsterdam, before continuing to his destination. He still could not muster a sense of immediacy about the appointment: perhaps the secret meetings were beginning to bore him or else he might have expected a new mission in Israel where he no longer felt secure. Then again Hugo could have had a kind of sixth sense warning that all might not be well. Herrmann's long absence without a mesage or a call was inexplicable. In the back of his mind these were serious fears, but he pushed them aside as he approached Vienna. He had been twenty-nine years a spy. Next year it would be three decades. That was enough for any man. Maybe that would be discussed, too, at the meeting in Vienna: that the trail had come to an end at last, and the Russians understood this. In the second week of October he embarked on the final stretch of his uncertain journey to Austria.

Before Hugo left England, Paul may have received news from KGB headquarters that Herrmann was no longer reliable. From Herrmann in New York, the KGB knew, it was but a short step to the professor in Quebec City. The Soviets had now to think of him as expendable. All that was left was an uncertain propaganda victory if he followed all the other important Western defectors to the East. But Hugo, living in his mysterious world of frantic travel and illusion, told himself, like others before him, that no one could ever find proof of his espionage activities. He did not believe anyone could be interested in his NATO period twenty years ago. Through the KGB Hugo had discovered the adventure that eluded him in World War II—and had made an effort to satisfy the craving to put his mark in his own way on the affairs of the world. He had partially succeeded. But the fate that now awaited him was uncertain.

Meanwhile the Yugoslavian embassy in Paris told the professor he would be allowed into Yugoslavia without harassment from the police, providing he came as a tourist and did not remain longer than forty-eight hours. Lili waited in Belgrade, and for her he was willing to make personal sacrifices. With these preparations made, Hugo went to Vienna to talk to Paul.

The Vienna meeting was not held in the regular café near the Hochstadtplatz. Instead it took place in a handsome Mercedes sedan drawn up near the wall where the chalk-mark signals were written indicating the rendezvous. In the backseat of the vehicle Hugo sat with an impatient Paul, annoyed at the length of time it had taken the Canadian to arrive in Vienna. Behind in another car were other KGB personnel, and loitering across the street were Russian agents who seemed to have staked out the area. Hugo, once in the car with the KGB officer, suppressed a sudden spasm of panic. Something obviously was wrong. Although agitated, Paul kept his voice low, controlled with effort. But not a moment was wasted.

"You are in danger," he said immediately. "Correspondence has been intercepted, and you may be under surveillance. Herrmann is no longer reliable."

There was a shock of disbelief in Hugo's initial reaction, but Paul's silent, stern stare of disapproval left no room for doubt.

"You may still have a chance," Paul continued. "Accept the risk and cease henceforth all communication. Destroy the decoder, burn the one-time pads and yellow notebooks and any other evidence."

"I couldn't," Hugo protested. "It is all distributed between Paris, Ottawa and Quebec City."

Then Paul gave Hugo the alternative.

"Defect now. You will be safe in Moscow. I am leaving for Bratislava immediately. You can come with me if you wish."

Hugo, contrary to what he said later, seriously considered this option, but there were personal reasons for refusing. Lili was waiting in Belgrade. His mother was in Ottawa and so were his children. He had a special affection for his youngest son, now ten years old. He could not possibly leave for Russia without making some prior arrangements. And he didn't absolutely believe the dramatic urgings of Paul. The Russians always exaggerated. They were obsessive people. And their manic fears could change from hour to hour. Aside from this, Hugo's world was made partly out of the stuff of dreams. The illusion persisted that after thirty years in the KGB nothing much could happen to him. Somehow he would find a way to get through this period on his own. Therefore he declined Paul's offer to defect. When he was ready—if the time ever came—he knew how to make the arrangements himself. Paul gave Hugo his final money: eight thousand dollars. This could help him with some of his expenses. Then he said a warm and perhaps sentimental good-bye and drove off in the Mercedes. Hugo never saw his friend Paul again.

After this meeting, he was suddenly engulfed by a sense of immense relief. Then, slowly, uncertainty mixed with a little bit of sadness replaced this feeling. He had said farewell to a friend whom he had known for twenty-one years. It was a long friendship, and the parting was tinged with a kind of bitter-sweet nostalgia.

In spite of the warnings from Paul, Hugo travelled that month to Jidda to doggedly complete his research on the petro-chemical industry in the gulf states. He spent several weeks there and then returned to Paris, where he collected a car and motored to Belgrade to visit with Lili. This sabbatical year was one of constant travel. And as he moved about Europe it was difficult to believe that he travelled only for himself. He could never wipe out all traces of his activities with the KGB. It was almost as if this journey was his own personal farewell to all those cities and places he had visited, not as a tourist, but as a seeker of intelligence on behalf of an alien power.

In Belgrade with Lili, Hugo gave her a portion of the money received from Paul and asked her to write a letter to his Quebec address saying she was undergoing vital treatment for an incurable cancer. He was burning traces of evidence and attempting to establish a story that could explain his activities. But it was difficult to undo in a few months a lifetime of deception and espionage.

In the spring Hugo had a final look at his lovely villa in Spain in the hills of Mijas. He could not do more than look at it because his agent in Malaga had rented it again for five more years at a still ridiculously low figure. The apartment in Torremolinos was available for several months, and he stayed there working on his petro-chemical paper, now and then travelling to Paris and Madrid. Then Hugo returned to London. He had left a suitcase, some books and personal papers in the Barbican flat. While he was there he did his utmost to revive his London contact but was unable to do so. Instead he left a message in the British Museum at a pre-arranged place on one of the book stacks.

For most of the summer of 1979 he commuted between the Continent and London. He spent quite a bit of time on the south coast of England in the small yachting centres, preparing for a sailing course he wished to take to obtain his yachtmaster certificate. Then he returned to Canada, his sabbatical coming to an end. In his own mind certain contingency plans had taken shape. Whether these plans would be put into effect would depend on what, if anything, awaited him upon his return to Quebec. His European journeys during the year 1978-1979 were almost impossible to track. Passport entries reveal repeated trips to almost every major European capital. But it is known that he had more than one passport; therefore it is impossible to know whether he travelled east behind the Iron Curtain during that critical year of 1979. But he was making plans, examining the options. If the situation was as desperate as Paul had said, sooner or later he would have to make a decision.

The professor started teaching again at Laval in the 1979

university year. He thought that perhaps his spy career had quietly ended the way he had wanted it to, without fuss or attention. And that Paul had exaggerated the danger. Lili Galeva was now out of his life, Paul had sunk forever into the grey mists of Russian life, and Herrmann was no more. As a souvenir, a memento of his past to remind him of the people who were becoming no more than a fading legend, he kept the metal decoder. Almost a year had elapsed since Paul had issued the stern warning in Vienna to defect. That was all part of the grand illusion. None of it had really happened.

– CHAPTER ELEVEN –

The Interrogation

1979 - 1982

At 7.13 a.m. on November 4, 1979, the fatal knock sounded on the door of apartment 208 at 2445 St. Foy. The professor was preparing his lectures for the day. When he opened the door, three plainclothes officers, led by redheaded Inspector Frank Pratt of the Royal Canadian Mounted Police, stood outside.

"Professor Hambleton?" Pratt asked, identifying himself.

"Yes," Hugo answered calmly, almost thankfully.

"We have a search warrant for your apartment."

Gazing at the three men standing in the doorway, Hugo understood. No further explanations were necessary. Thus began the ordeal that ended the spy's career.

The apartment was thoroughly searched for more than eight hours. Documents, notebooks, papers and the decoder were seized and removed in a large cardboard box to RCMP headquarters in Quebec City. The Mounties did not arrest him but they took away his passports. He could attend his classes that day but would be picked up when the last class ended and driven to his first interview.

The next day the Hambleton house in Ottawa was raided. A radio and important documents were found, some belonging to the Canadian Privy Council.

At his first interview at RCMP Quebec headquarters Hugo was shown the video tape of Herrmann sitting alone behind a wooden table, answering questions. During the interview the defector admitted he had been a KGB agent in America for twelve years and had known the professor as a trusted KGB agent much of that time. Herrmann deeply and irrevocably implicated the professor in the American KGB operation. His evidence was detailed, clear, conclusive, and quite overwhelming. The question remained, however, whether it was all admissible in a courtroom.

From the beginning Hugo talked freely. But what the Mounties did not know was that his voluminous disclosures were limited to what he had decided to tell and what could be revealed by Herrmann. There was much that he omitted. He failed to disclose his activities prior to 1962, a period with which Herrmann was unfamiliar. In the first series of interviews the NATO years were never once mentioned. (Neither the professor nor the Mounties disclosed everything they knew.) Hugo was very careful during these first thirteen interrogations. Frequently he wouldn't answer a question but would write it down and come back at the next meeting with the details.

Inspector Pratt showed photographs of a meeting between Hugo and an unidentified person in an Ottawa bookstore on Elgin Street after he had returned to Canada. Here he was seen to insert sheets of paper containing a message into the pages of a book. Moments later a stranger arrived, surreptitiously removed the papers and left the store. Hugo was also photographed arriving at several of his dead-letter drops outside Montreal near the hunting lodge. He could be observed on one occasion disappearing into a wood, picking up an object near a tree, and then returning to his car. The professor was a cooperative and apparently willing subject, but answered all questions with such liberal additions of fact and fiction that the interrogators spent most of their time trying to unravel the many strands of his involved stories.

Sometimes the routine of questioning varied. Instead of interviewing him at RCMP headquarters, he might be taken to his own apartment or a hotel room. But the method of questioning was undeviating. Where it finished one day, it would begin again at the next meeting, as they slowly went over every year of his adult life. The sessions lasted as long as four, sometimes five hours. In Montreal, interviews were sometimes held in the Holiday Inn and Ruby Foo's Motor Hotel. The subjects ranged over a wide area, and Hugo continued to tell the Mounties only what he thought would best serve his own purpose, which was to protect himself as much as possible. Volumes of information were mistaken for quality.

The technique of interrogation that the security service employed with the professor was to match the detailed profile of his known life against the story he unfolded. Whenever discrepancies occurred, the interrogators would limit their questions to the obvious differences in the testimony and thus hope to break down their subject.

In the interviews Hugo seemed to be more than a match for his interrogators. He was calm, never lost his composure over many months, and led his inquisitors up dead-end streets and into a fictitious world where they more than once lost their way. He spoke so volubly without any desire to be restrained, acted so friendly, that after a number of meetings everyone was on first-name terms. The Mounties couldn't become annoyed at the modest, frugally living, pleasant professor. Personally they liked him. To do their job more effectively, a little anger would have helped. They couldn't even insult him; when they asked him why he didn't bathe more often because he smelled, he simply laughed and treated it as a joke. Pratt and McIlroy were old hands at interrogations. But they were plodders: they knew only one way to go, asking question after question hoping for some incriminating disclosure whereby the criminal investigation officer, McIlroy, could charge the subject.

A number of tactics were utilized by both Hugo and the RCMP. The security service put out information to their special newspaper reporters who for a few small favours from the RCMP agreed to leak choice bits of news on Hugo to the public. And as Hugo related: "There was press reporting put out by the security service. They told me themselves about this. And some I put out. I encouraged it to give the impression I worked against the Russians."

Finally, after thirteen sessions with the security service, in early 1980 Hugo was shown a communication signed by the solicitor general of Canada. He was allowed to read it but not to keep it. It was addressed to Professor Hugh Hambleton. In exchange for immunity from prosecution, he was asked to give his cooperation to the security services. This he readily agreed to do.

The Mountie who presented this immunity communication could scarcely disguise his contempt as he read the document. Some weeks earlier a lengthy report sent by McIlroy to the Justice Department in Ottawa was thought to possess more than sufficient evidence for an effective prosecution. The RCMP were deeply disappointed at the news of the immunity offer. They were out for blood. In spite of the friendly interrogations and the first-name terms, they had the pride of the force to protect. They wanted Hugo.

But a decision had been made by the Liberal government that insufficient grounds under the Official Secrets Act existed to take action. Solicitor General Robert Kaplan, whose office received all telex correspondence from the RCMP, concluded that Hambleton could best serve the cause of justice by cooperating with the security service. In turn there would be no prosecution.*

The denial of prosecution was like a personal affront to the security service. They wished to embarrass the government and the solicitor general, and they set out to do just that.

Kaplan later denied that a deal had been offered, and it is possible that no real letter of immunity existed, that the document shown to Hugo was a fake designed to lull the suspect into a false sense of security. But while the letter conveniently vanished in Canada, its existence was confirmed by the attorney general of the United Kingdom at the Old Bailey two years later. And if immunity was not offered, why was there no move to prosecute? After each taped interview with Hugo the transcripts were sent to the solicitor general. If he read them, he had to know the weight of evidence the RCMP had amassed.

After the so-called immunity deal the interviews became largely covert in hotel rooms in Montreal and Quebec City. The security service were convinced that the professor had consciously misled them to hide a more serious phase in his espionage career. With immunity they rightly guessed he would be more inclined to talk about matters that previously had been avoided. The interviews therefore continued. The RCMP would not give up, and their subject willingly complied, a condition of the immunity which he believed had been honourably given.

The interrogators decided they would now concentrate on events that happened prior to 1962. They would go back as far as the end of World War II in the hope of finding something worthwhile. Unbeknownst to Hugo the security service had put out a few inquiries in Europe about his NATO service. Coincidentally they learned that the years of his employment there, between 1956 and 1961, was a period when the KGB had almost access-at-will to that organization's documents. The coincidence was worth further investigation. To the pleasure and amazement

---

* Alan Lawrence, solicitor general in the short-lived Conservative government, later declared he had briefly investigated the Hambleton file but that he had had no time to weigh the evidence and act before he was out of office.

of the RCMP the professor, convinced he would be protected everywhere from prosecution, began to disclose the story of his NATO years.

Almost all of the results of Hugo's interrogations were sent overseas. MI5, along with the French intelligence service, was given a complete dossier.

During this interlude of investigation in Quebec, a senior officer of the French intelligence service known as the DST (Direction de la Sécurité de Territoire) arrived on the scene. In his possession was a series of twenty-five photographs, and the professor was asked to identify the individuals portrayed. Included were pictures of many senior French Army officers. There is no doubt that the information Hugo divulged and the identifications he was able to make made a substantial contribution to the intelligence services of the West. As the RCMP began to realize the dimension of their discoveries, they actually worried for the professor's safety. On two separate occasions they strongly suggested he accept their protection, which he refused.

In May of 1980 Hugo was allowed to go to England to attend a conference at Exeter University and to present a paper dealing with the petro-chemical industry in Saudi Arabia. Although this was later denied by the British Special Branch, he did receive an invitation from Professor Al Malleck and another from Timothy Niblock of the Arab and Islamic studies department of Exeter.

At that conference he met an ethnic Russian and an Indian who lived in Moscow with whom he was able to establish contact. He gave the Indian a verbal message to be delivered to his East Berlin contact address.

While Hugo was in London he underwent a brief interrogation by two Special Branch detectives, one of whom was Superintendent Peter Westcott from the Rochester Row police station. The meeting was courteous and friendly. The Canadian knew he was under surveillance and was thus unable to meet the one contact who was essential for setting in motion one last adventure. Unable to see this man, he returned to Quebec immediately after the conference to avoid any suspicion.

Twenty minutes after he entered his apartment in Quebec City the telephone rang. Interrogator Pratt was on the line wanting to know all the details of his stay in the United Kingdom. An interview was scheduled for the following day. There would be no end to the questioning.

In Canada Hugo was a free man. At Laval University he had become a celebrity, not a person to be despised but rather a figure of mystery regarded with awe by students and faculty alike. The professor's classes were among the most popular in the university, and he found that people who had once ignored him were now going out of their way to greet him. Strangers would say hello. The life of anonymity he had always sought now belonged to the past.

Phone calls came from newspapers across Canada. But his fame still remained local. In the foreign press he rated only a small column on an inside page. No matter how much Canadians had to say about their spies, the outside world was not interested all that much in Canadian espionage activities. Some questions were raised in the House of Commons by that diligent spy hunter and self-appointed guardian of Canada's security, the late Thomas Cossett, but after a few days Hugo was dropped by the press. After all, a spy in which no foreign newspaper showed interest could not be important.

The Canadian government apparently reweighed the evidence of the Hambleton case with care and came again to the conclusion there was insufficient proof to proceed under the Official Secrets Act.

The security service sometimes regularly, sometimes intermittently, continued to interview Hugo, who was a model of cooperation and gentility. To his university students and staff, he jokingly referred to himself as a "part-time spy." According to the law of the land a man was only guilty of a crime when convicted, but no trial was contemplated, no prosecution was readied, and Hugo had more than satisfied his inquisitors by filling their tapes and notepads with a torrent of information that was now being sifted and evaluated and shared with other friendly intelligence services.

Unnoticed by the RCMP, Hugo was tiring of the constant surveillance and interrogation. The wear and tear was beginning to tell. For thirty years he had not disclosed a word of his work to a single person, and now, it seemed, he was telling everyone almost everything; although as much as he told, much still lay untold. But the RCMP never gave up. They believed that prosecution had been withheld for political reasons. At the Ruskin home of the Hambletons classified papers belonging to the Canadian Privy Council had been found, as well as NATO documents. No one has ever answered the question, Who gave Hugo the Privy Council documents? The answer could prove to be an embarrassment for someone very high in the government hierarchy. The position the Mounties took was that they had more evidence than required for prosecution, certainly more than had been necessary in past investigations. The feeling in the security service was that someone in the Privy Council, or very close to it, was being protected. This suspicion still exists.

Of all Hugo's children, his youngest son, George William, was the dearest to him. He resembled his father in every way. Now a tall, gangling, awkward, bashful boy of fourteen, he loved his father deeply and would always love him no matter what happened. Hugo decided to take a risk that would involve his son. Together they would succeed or fail.

After his visit to Exeter in the summer of 1980 Hugo had failed to make contact with the man he waited for in London. But he would make one more effort, whatever the risk. To do this he required an elaborate cover story for another trip to England. Pratt had warned him more than once that not only would he be unwelcome should he go to the United Kingdom, but that more dire consequences could await him. The madness of such a course of action was hard to justify. The countries to which he could travel in safety, without fear of arrest, were limited. He risked detention in France, interrogation in Spain and the same fate in Belgium. Mistakenly, he believed he could rely on English tolerance for the same immunity from prosecution that Canadians had offered in exchange for information. He would be tempting fate and British tolerance to the limits of endurance, and he knew this. But he decided he had to take the chance.

He was planning to defect, to seek asylum in Russia. There was nowhere else to go. Although superficially life in Quebec City appeared more or less normal, in reality Hugh dwelt in a kind of living hell. Each morning from habit he rose regularly at seven for his classes. Each evening he religiously prepared his lectures. On weekends he visited his mother and children in Ottawa. He followed a seldom deviating routine. He had few visitors and infrequently left the sanctuary of his living quarters once he arrived home in the evening.

Only his adherence to a strict routine saved his sanity, for inwardly he was in a state of great turmoil and disorientation. The RCMP kept him like a puppet on a string, jerking it at will whenever they wished. The suspense was nerve-wracking: the questioning might stop for a few weeks or a month, then without warning begin again. It might be prompted by a request from a foreign intelligence service or the RCMP might be curious about a matter which upon re-examination didn't stand up to close scrutiny. The security service would never be finished with him as long as he still had a drop of information that could be squeezed out.

Hugo was much stronger than he looked. But the continuous interviews were deeply disruptive to the simple lifestyle he was now trying to maintain. In November of 1981, he removed the phone from his apartment in St. Foy and also at his mother's home in Ottawa. But he couldn't cut off communication at his office in Laval.

Although the Canadian government had decided not to prosecute, the security service of the RCMP acted as if they had not heard the news. On their own they continued to investigate, never relieving the pressure. Although there appeared to be no overt malice in the RCMP interviews, there was a menacing undertone that was persistent and exhausting. The Mounties might question with a lack of aggression, but their memory was savage. They forgot nothing. And by this time they were really out for more than the professor; they were after bigger game.

Like most security services, the Mounties had become experts at the "planted" story, the "dirty trick," the "break-in," the use of the "wire tap," blackmail and surveillance. These things were tools of the trade in the murky twilight zone in which they operated. Elected officials deliberately avoided this dirty and repulsive world and preferred to know as little as possible about it. In Hugo's case the less the solicitor general had to know the more pleased he became. The RCMP found their minister naïve, incapable of understanding their task as a counter-espionage agency. Kaplan was confused, plunged into a subject beyond his depth. The Mounties fed him what was most convenient and did not inform him about many aspects of the investigation until it was almost concluded. When Kaplan had all the facts, he decided the best course of action was to do nothing. Before him, Justice Minister Jean Chrétien had had similar sentiments, and the Conservative solicitor general, Alan Lawrence, had pleaded the brevity of his term in office for his inaction. But all this did not matter. The politicians did not direct the Hambleton show. It was done by the RCMP in their own time and their own way. They were the only people who had all the knowledge and the continuity of power, and they used it in a style best suited to themselves.

If the interrogators had been more perceptive and sensitive, they might have detected clues to the slow disintegration of Hugo's personality taking place before their eyes. But they were not great psychologists. On the other hand, to an observer, even a man like Pratt, the signs were difficult to read. The exterior of the professor was imperturbable. He had learned long ago to mask his feelings, his true facial expressions, to act with assured mannerisms regardless of what the effort cost him.

In the interview sessions his answers rambled. The response to a simple question could take ten minutes. He often wandered aimlessly into all sorts of subjects: his sister, his students, Lili Galeva's imaginary illness, his desire to learn to sail, the character of the Russians he had met in all parts of the world. Sergeant McIlroy guessed correctly when he suggested that for every one fact that Hugo revealed, he hid ten more that were deeply compromising. But the RCMP were not the KGB. They could only ask and intimidate; they could not use torture. But as Hugo would say more than once, the deadly questions asked by Torquemada, the Spanish Inquisitor of the fifteenth century, were also an exquisite, agonizing form of torture.

In spite of this slow breakdown there was a tough core in Hugo. He had something of his mother in him. He could take punishment, take the intense grilling. He had a formula: he spoke torrents, truth and fiction. The note-takers could not keep up with him.

Despite his outward appearance the desire to break out was growing inside him with a passionate but controlled intensity. In the spring of 1982, he decided to risk all with his long-prepared scheme. Every move was rehearsed in his mind. Not a word was mentioned to any member of his family. All he needed was time. Four days of freedom in England would be enough.

Hugo's trip to England would not be motivated by the "reverse psychology" theory stated by the solicitor general of Canada. Nor did the Canadian security service warn Hugo against going to England out of the goodness of their hearts; when the time came for justice, the RCMP wanted to be responsible for administering that justice themselves. They did not have too much confidence in the British intelligence service. It was common knowledge the British had a long history of traitors concealed within their service for many years down to the present day. Besides, the RCMP team that had investigated the professor since 1978 felt much more at home in America and much closer to the CIA than they did to the British. And the CIA shared the Canadians' distrust of MI5.

In 1982 more evidence was being accumulated, and a new trap was set for him on the American continent. The CIA and the RCMP wanted Hugo in the United States. One of the ruses was to have him accept an invitation to deliver a lecture on Saudi Arabia at the Center for International and Strategic Studies at

Georgetown University in Washington. Hugo knew that if he travelled to Washington the FBI would arrest him. Herrmann had supplied sufficient evidence. So he did not fall into the trap. As he said, "It would have been a one-way trip to Washington."

The way Hugo chose to leave his lifetime career as a spy was through England. The indications were that he might be closely interrogated in that country, but all he needed was forty-eight hours for the apparatus of defection to be set in motion and two further days of grace. England was his only hope.

When he went his son would go with him. The story Hugo told the RCMP, and anyone else who asked, was that he wanted to show the boy Europe, and go sailing with him on the south coast. One of the towns on the south coast from which ferries and hover-craft departed for Holland and the Baltic would be the perfect point of embarkation. With the throngs of summer tourists he would go on a regular scheduled ferry service unnoticed. If, however, he came under very close surveillance a small boat could be chartered. There were dozens of ports of departure from which a man could vanish. Hundreds of small private yachts crossed the Channel daily. The commodity Hugo required most of all was time and the assistance of his friends.

Chance would be an essential element in the success or failure of the flight to Russia. If he could elude the Canadian security service and the British, it would be a great personal triumph and the last great romantic adventure of his career. The grand finale. Hugo honestly believed he had nothing more to lose.

On June 18, Inspector Frank Pratt met Hugo for the last time at the Skyline Hotel in Montreal, categorically warning him to stay in Canada. Once in England and detained by the British Special Branch, he would be out of the RCMP jurisdiction at a time when the security official considered the case but half-completed. But the RCMP lacked the authority to detain him or confiscate his passport. He didn't believe much of what Hugo had told him about the purpose of his hazardous European trip and really had no idea why the professor had chosen this summer to go to Europe despite warnings. But Pratt, steady and uninspired, did not really understand his subject, nor could he guess at the hidden reserves still left.

Hugo felt that chance had caught him. Perhaps chance might deliver him. After all this time, he would never admit to Pratt how painful, sometimes torturous, the interrogations had become. Hugo remained intractable. He would go to London. Pratt and others went as far as they dared to dissuade Hugo from making the trip, but it was all to no avail. Hugo said, "I have nothing to be afraid of," and added, "I have bought the tickets, and they are non-refundable." He was told the loss of money would be preferable to the loss of his freedom.

Hugo arrived with his son at London's Heathrow Airport on the morning of June 23, 1982. Before he left Quebec City he gave Pratt his itinerary, which showed a proposed visit to Paris on July 6 and seventh. Hugo claimed later that he had scheduled meetings with French security officials, but this is most unlikely. He was not anxious to go back to France, but it was a good story. He also insisted that his French handler, the imaginary Jean Masson, would be waiting for him when he arrived in Paris. Torremolinos was also on the travel schedule, as well as an expected interview with the Spanish security service, which was eager to ask a number of questions. These were Hugo's professed intentions.

He carried with him twelve copies of his manuscript on King Alfonso of Spain. He had more research to do at the British Museum. He was taking elaborate precautions to make his London trip seem like an innocent working holiday with his son.

As Hugo and the boy disembarked from the plane and walked toward the immigration desks, he was not surprised to hear his name paged on the public-address system. When he made himself known, he was confronted by two detectives from London Special Branch. The man whose responsibility it was to meet and caution him was Superintendent Peter Westcott. Westcott later claimed he had never heard of the professor until that morning. The Canadian was told that if he entered the United Kingdom he could be subject to prosecution. Westcott gave him the choice of entering the country by passing the immigration barrier or waiting in the transit lounge for the next available plane back. Hugo politely declined the offer to return to Canada and said he preferred to pass through immigration with his son. It was a carefully considered risk. He discussed the matter in a civilized fashion at length with Westcott, sitting on a divan in a deserted section of the immigration area, while his son observed the intrusion into his anticipated holiday, uncomprehending.

Westcott allowed Hugo to leave the airport once he decided not to return home but asked him to make himself available should he be needed. This was agreed. After collecting his baggage Hugo took a taxi to the Overseas League on Park Place in London's West End where accommodations had been reserved.

The meeting at Heathrow had been bizarre. It was quite beyond Westcott's comprehension why a man who was told he might be held for prosecution should not turn around and go home a free man, given the opportunity. Westcott now was forced to confer with his superiors, since he had not anticipated that the Canadian would ignore his caution. The instructions Westcott eventually received had to come from Sir Michael Havers, the British attorney general. And because of the considerable political implications, Havers had to have the advice of the Prime Minister's Office. What no one suspected was Hugo's reason for coming to the United Kingdom. No one in England knew of the inner turmoil, the powerful motivation that drove Hugo to escape.

Since the RCMP had lost their man, they must give every appearance of having planned the deliverance of the spy into the waiting British hands. They had to alter their policy. Now they would have to tell all. If Hugo's deliverance to the British should blow up in their faces, the Canadian solicitor general would have a lot of explaining to do in Parliament. The RCMP interrogators concluded that the professor had no feelings, no normal responses, no real family affections. If he had any, why would he take his son with him when he was aware he could be arrested? There was a coldness in the character they were unable to fathom.

On their first day in London, father and son took a double-decker bus around London. Hugo became a sightseer, but one with a desperate sense of urgency. The two of them lunched on sausages and tea near Picadilly. They walked down Leicester Square to Great Russell Street and stood before the vast British Museum but did not pass through the great iron gates into the grounds. Hugo couldn't detect any surveillance but knew that he was being watched. The Special Branch would not be that indifferent to his movements. Everything now depended on a message communicated to one of the Russians he had met at Exeter on the previous summer. Its transmission was imperative. Hugo was certain the message had been received in East Berlin. But would it be acted upon? He was sure Paul would not fail him in the final hour.

On the buses, on the crowded streets, in the cafés and along the embankment Hugo searched for a familiar face, some sign of recognition, an old password that had been exchanged at one of the métro stations in Paris or at the Hochstadtplatz in Vienna. But none came. No contact was made on June 24. Perhaps his man was frightened and waited. If the KGB felt they were under too great a risk in England, then Hugo had two other places to go: West Berlin and Vienna.

Everything depended on whether the British were serious. If the British Official Secrets Act was interpreted in the same manner as the Canadian one, he could visualize no good reason for being detained. Hugo could not anticipate why he should be further interrogated in England when he had been interviewed in Canada for a period of almost three years. He knew his story from memory. It bored him. He hated it. Passionately he sought some way of removing it altogether from his mind. But there was none. Others would never be satisfied. And perhaps when his interrogators found the truth, they would seek something beyond that.

By nightfall on June 24 it became apparent the KGB had deserted him. But he still refused to believe the desertion was permanent. Perhaps they were waiting for the right moment. Hugo decided to leave London the next day for the coast without exciting attention and made preparations. He would not check out of the hotel. He said not a word to his son as he put the boy to bed that night and packed his bags. A rented car was parked outside the club at his disposal. In three hours Hugo could be at Southampton and catch the hovercraft to France. That was all that was left.

But Westcott moved too swiftly.

Early in the morning the Special Branch officer came to the Overseas League. He had finally received instructions from higher authority. The professor was to be detained for questioning at the Rochester Row police station. Interrogation commenced twenty-five minutes after the Canadian was driven to his destination. Altogether, Westcott interviewed him six times between June 25 and June 27, in cooperation with the unseen case officer assigned to Westcott from MI5. Some of the sessions lasted as long as seven hours. Two hundred and sixty-four pages of testimony were accumulated, and every page of testimony was read back and signed by Hugo, who wrote his signature dutifully without looking too closely at what had been typed. The interviews were not on a first-name basis, as they had been in Canada. They were formal—courteous, but cold. Hugo was referred to only as Mr. Hambleton.

During the course of his detention Hugo learned happily that his son had been put in the care of Miss M.C. Kelly of the

Canadian High Commissioner's Office in London, and she had arranged for him to live with the family of one of the Canadian officials.

On June 27 the Canadian was brought by police van to the Horseferry Road magistrate's court where the presiding magistrate, Edmund McDermott, charged him under Section I of the 1911 Official Secrets Act. He was denied bail "because of the nature and gravity of the offence [and] the belief that he would fail to surrender." From here the prisoner was sent to a high-security wing of Brixton Prison on Jebb Avenue in the southeast of London to await trial.

Of Brixton Hugo would say: "Being here, apart from the piquant novelty, is useful in that it is relaxing and allows me to get the best in radio programs. Now we are in the middle of the proms at the Royal Albert Hall. One sad note is that I would have been passing the week with my son, sailing in the Channel, working my way to a competent skipper certificate. Now I am listening to the shipping forecast. It says, 'Gale eight, increasing to severe gale nine.'"

- CHAPTER TWELVE -

The
Trial

December 1982

The number one criminal court at the Old Bailey is a grim, foreboding place. In the gallery the hard, narrow wooden benches are as austere as church pews and polished from the bottoms of countless visitors over the century. A high, cavernous ceiling hangs like a canopy of gloom over the dimly lit courtroom. Visitors look down on the proceedings huddled in the small dark alcove-like gallery about twenty feet above the dock where the prisoner stands alone enclosed by a wooden stockade.

On this day, November 29, sitting on tiered benches against the far wall were the ten men and two women of the jury, silent and watchful. Perhaps normally they might have been a little resentful at being called away from some pressing work for jury duty. But they knew they were involved in a spectacle, with ringside seats to view the proceedings and an essential role to play in dispensing justice. This trial was an opportunity not to be missed. The Hambleton case had received enormous publicity in the press. An air of excitement could be felt in the courtroom as participants and spectators alike waited anxiously for justice to unfold.

In the far corner near the jury, under a canopy, was the witness box. Close at hand at his desk sat the shorthand stenographer. On a dias, above all the other participants, was Justice David Powell Croom-Johnson in a white grotesque wig. The judge was a man of experience, forbidding in his black gown, with a large open ledger before him, pen in hand as if about to inscribe a doomsday notice. Only one instrument of authority was placed higher than Croom-Johnson. Directly above the judge, secured to the wall, was the massive silver sword of justice dating from the thirteenth century. Below the judge's dias, attired solemnly in his funereal robes, was the clerk of the court.

Across the wide expanse of empty courtroom floor, almost directly below the balcony was the long table where the defence barrister, John Lloyd-Eley Q.C. sat with an assistant, Mr. C. De Silva. Next to him was Edward Wein, Hugo's solicitor, a small fat man with a moustache who had prepared the case for the barrister. This was the big case of Wein's life, and he was determined to make the most out of it. Not more than a few feet from the defence was the prosecutor, Sir Michael Havers, the British attorney general. His presence for the prosecution was an undeniable signal that the British intended to show no mercy. Sir Michael had two assistants, a Mr. R. Amyot and a Mr. J. Bevan.

The cast was large, extravagant, with no expenses spared. The government was paying the bill. The witnesses who waited in a room upstairs to be called were from the security services of Canada, England and France.

Hugo's solicitor had already flown to Paris and Ottawa. He had requested twenty thousand dollars from the Hambleton family, but they had no money to pay him. The family was hopeful that British legal aid would come to the rescue. No one, however, seemed concerned with such mundane things as money during the trial. British justice demands the accused be defended, and this had been arranged. The solicitor general wanted no delays, and nothing was going to deter him from carrying out his instructions. He was under orders to proceed with the utmost haste so that his government could rescue what was left of the tarnished reputation of the intelligence service.

The British were out to demonstrate their house of spies would be cleaned. However, almost all the important English spies had been granted immunity in exchange for the information they had given. Several had escaped, and the remainder were dead or in Russia. So a born and bred Canadian was suddenly given dual nationality and made to look British. Anyone with a British parent could do the same thing. The press and the court appeared determined to do their damnedest to portray Hambleton as an Englishman. And those seven days in December would be made to look like the trial of the century. Orders had come down from the Prime Minister's Office itself. What the Canadians could not finish, the British must.

In the brown musty air, under the dull light in the lofty hall, among all the white unsmiling faces, justice was about to ceremoniously be served. The pageantry was extraordinarily impressive to a stranger. But the conclusion of this ritual was already known to the defence and the prosecution. Hugo in his voluminous admissions during interrogation had given all the material any reasonably astute lawyer needed. But the show had to go on.

No one can stage a ceremony better than the British can, after centuries of practice. The clerk of the court read out the charge as the performance began:

> That between September 4, 1956, and October 31, 1961, for purposes prejudicial to the safety or interest of the United Kingdom he communicated to a Russian agent information, namely top secret, secret and confidential material belonging to the North Atlantic Treaty Organization, which was calculated to be, or might have been or was intended to be directly or indirectly useful to an enemy.

> That between September 1, 1956, and November 5, 1979, for a purpose prejudicial to the safety and interest of the United Kingdom he obtained information which was calculated to be, or might have been or was intended to be directly or indirectly useful to an enemy.

Hugo pleaded not guilty to both charges.

The Crown presented its case methodically. Peter Westcott read excerpts from the Special Branch interrogations. A communications expert, who remained unidentified, explained how the Russian decoder worked. The jury was told, *in camera*, the nature of the NATO documents photographed by the defendant. The defence barrister, John Lloyd-Eley, over the two days of December 2 and third, a Thursday and a Friday, put his client on the stand and took him through his entire life history. There were several reasons for doing this. One was to illustrate that the defendant had committed no crime on British soil. Another was to expand upon a distinguished career of service to his country in peace and to the Allied cause in war. If Lloyd-Eley and Wein had done their homework more thoroughly, they would have omitted Hugo's military career. The witness gave a vivid and exaggerated account of his military record, stating he served behind the enemy lines in France carrying out intelligence missions.

The defendant's academic background, his parents' history, were brought into evidence. It really sounded impressive. The qualifications were those of an outstanding scholar and public servant. But the Canadian grew gradually more digressive, his answers wandered aimlessly. He was forgetful and frequently was reminded by the judge of the question asked.

Lloyd-Eley, a middle-aged, sometimes irascible man, frequently lost his patience with the long-winded responses of his own client. But under the best of conditions it would certainly have been an uphill fight for the defence unless something spectacular had been produced to offset the testimony of Westcott and the possible testimony of RCMP officers, who were also available to the prosecution.

Then the defendant himself suddenly supplied the spectacular. He claimed to be a triple agent working for the KGB, the Canadians and the French. Jean Masson was named as his French handler, and Jacques La Liberté, referred to as "C," became his man in Canada. This invention was difficult to sustain, and in any event the prosecution had to demolish any story that would interfere with a successful case. Toward the end of Lloyd-Eley's second day of examination, Hugo descended down a one-way street. He was led there inadvertently by his own barrister, whom one might have believed was working for the prosecution. The question asked referred to an answer he had given to his Special Branch investigator in London. It concerned his motivation for reputedly acting for the Russians, and it was extremely damaging.

"I suppose," Hugo said in reply, "you could call it a lack of will power, unable to break a relationship. Again when I came back from Moscow, there was a strong sense of not wanting to be involved, but then there is a certain sense of excitement. There is a certain camaraderie with a person who is looking after you—Paul for instance. You get the feeling you are playing an important role." Then he went on to say in answer to whether he had any ideological or political convictions about communism, "I was not ideologically opposed after the war."

If Lloyd-Eley was attempting to give him cues, then his client missed all of them or he found it impossible to focus his mind any longer on the proceedings. Perhaps the Canadian had given up long before the cross-examination was to begin from Sir Michael.

Hugo testified that he had passed misinformation to the Russians. But the so-called "doctored" documents, which the defendant said he gave to the KGB on behalf of Jean Masson and the French, unfortunately could not be produced as evidence. They alone could prove the defendant to be a double agent. Lloyd-

Eley might have been doing his best, but the prosecution had all the artillery and what ammunition the defence had was limited. The Canadian's confused story of agents and counter-agents was falling apart, tangled in an enveloping web of half-truths and dialectics which Hugo wove about himself. It would have taken a more brilliant barrister than Lloyd-Eley to unravel the mess. When Friday, December 3, arrived, the prisoner was relieved to escape into the weekend and the solitude of his cell at Brixton.

On the following Monday, December 6, Lloyd-Eley dealt briefly with the last of six interviews by the Special Branch, making another effort to reduce the wealth of evidence against his client. But the dutiful efforts of Lloyd-Eley were wholly uninspired. The road uphill had grown almost vertical. It had become impossible to find extenuating circumstances in anything told to the Special Branch. And that was a repetition of what Hugo had told the RCMP. If he was not a Russian spy, he had to be a double agent and that evidence, even with the prompting of the defence, was confused and equivocal.

A last vain attempt was made by Lloyd-Eley to show the respectability of his client by introducing into the evidence the defendant's own description in the 1970-1972 editions of *Who's Who in Canada*. But this, alas, would be part of the unveiling of the prisoner.

Attorney General Sir Michael Havers began his cross-examination of Hugh Hambleton late on Monday morning, December 6.

Sir Michael would follow three avenues of attack. First, he would discredit the defendant's military record and thus throw into doubt the truth of all his testimony. Next he would set upon the double-agent story and demonstrate that the Canadian and French contacts who managed his relationships with the Russians were mere products of his imagination. Then he would force the professor to admit that he photographed NATO documents and passed the film to the Russians. If he did admit to this, there was only one conclusion to draw: Hugh George Hambleton was a spy.

Sir Michael, a shortish, powerfully built man with a thatch of white hair beneath his curled wig, was eager to set upon his victim. More than a hint of aggression dominated his courtroom behaviour. He had a superb theatrical sense and a dominating presence. As Her Majesty's attorney general since 1979, Sir Michael now had a unique opportunity to receive a vast amount of publicity that would help his political career if he was successful. He would be the loyal servant of the Crown who had convicted a major spy. And he didn't intend to lose a case in which the defendant had gratuitously provided all the evidence the Crown needed. All Sir Michael had to do was to hammer the nails home into the coffin.

Everything about Sir Michael's mood gave the impression of supreme confidence. As the principal actor on the stage, he would with consummate skill begin the dismemberment of the accused. Some of the titles of Sir Michael's publications—*The Rathenbury Murder, The Poisoned Life of Mrs. Maybrick*—had a flamboyant ring that was somehow consistent with the character himself. And behind Sir Michael stood the solid weight of authority and the sense of outrage the British people felt against an intelligence service that seemed to expose a new British traitor every few months. A devastating victory for Sir Michael would be a triumph for the Conservative government.

The media had helped create the creature on trial, and it would not be satisfied until the sacrifice had been made. There was, however, one difficulty an objective observer might have in understanding the trial. The accused was a Canadian. Most of the evidence had been originally supplied by the Canadian security service; Sir Michael continually referred to Inspector Frank Pratt by name. If the trial was so important, and the crime so deserving of attention, why wasn't the defendant back in Canada where he belonged? Extradition would have been a simple matter, and indeed welcomed by the British. The British didn't want the professor in the first place. Were there other reasons to keep the Canadian from being tried in his native land? After all, Canada was also a member of NATO. No one asked these questions.

Sir Michael in his cross-examination was shrewd, merciless. His tactics after the first few minutes became transparent. He began by exposing the tissue of half-truths and fabrications of the Canadian's war record. Before Sir Michael was a minute chronicle of the defendant's activities during almost every year of his adult life. In *Who's Who* he was listed as serving in the Allied Armies between 1943 and 1945, and he had told the court of his work behind the enemy lines with the French resistance movement. Unfortunately, Hugo had confirmed this under examination earlier by his own lawyer. But under intensive cross-examination by Sir Michael, the facts emerged.

"Let us get to the truth now. You did not even join up till February 1944 in America, did you? You never went to Algiers until four months after D-Day, October 25. It is not the sort of a great two years with the French."

Although caught out in one fabrication after another, the defendant maintained an extraordinary coolness. Or perhaps it was plain numbness, after being battered into a state of psychic unconsciousness. Hugo responded from reflexes without any real sense of life or emotion.

Once he was caught lying about his war record, it became a question whether the jury could believe anything else. The end was coming faster and easier than Sir Michael anticipated. Then the attorney general cleverly added one interesting aside hitherto unknown about the accused: according to his war record in the Free French Army the Canadian was accused of being pro-German. Astutely Hugo countered by saying, "I was pro-German but anti-Nazi." Even when responding by reflex he was difficult to corner. There were those rare moments at the beginning of the cross-examination when he acted as if he might be a match for Sir Michael. After all, he had endured three years of almost continuous questioning by some hard interrogators.

Later in the morning the prosecutor asked whether the accused had read what he signed when Special Branch Detective Sergeant Adams interrogated him. For the first time the Canadian's voice rose and faltered, the fear quite discernible.

"I don't know what you're driving at, sir. The officers can indicate. All right, I read them back. But I didn't read them back. Do you want me to say I read them when I didn't read them? You put pressure on me. Send me back to D block again."

It was hard for Sir Michael not to disguise a slight smile of satisfaction at his complete mastery over his wilting subject. Shortly thereafter, he obtained the admission that not only had the prisoner read back the transcripts of interrogation but had added and qualified parts of the testimony. On this foundation the attorney general quickly built the remainder of his case. He rapidly demolished the story that Hugo was a double agent with written denials by both the French and Canadian security services.

It was an unequal contest from the beginning. Hugo had been locked up for five months in a small cell and was thoroughly disorientated. Mentally he was sick, harassed, isolated from the other prisoners. He had no one to speak to most of the time except his warders, his interrogators and his examiners in court. Sir Michael arrived fresh from a good night's sleep onto centre stage of the Old Bailey with the eyes of the nation and the world press focussed upon him.

The attorney general played with his victim a little while

longer, not sure when he should deliver the final blow.

"You were telling Superintendent Westcott you passed classified documents to the Russians," Sir Michael said.

"Yes, sir."

Sir Michael was referring to the NATO period between 1956 and 1961.

"You had taken them home, photographed them, taken them back."

"Yes, sir."

Sir Michael in an ominous tone warned of the serious allegations the defendant had made earlier that he had spied in NATO at the behest of the French and Canadians. There *was* a Jean Masson, Sir Michael agreed, and Hugo did know him. But he was a fellow comrade who had served with the Canadian when he was briefly in Algeria with the Free French. The background of the accused had been painstakingly researched, combed over and over again by Sir Michael's staff for the minutest of details. Even the fictional creations had to be searched and refuted.

This was one spy who had supplied plenty of evidence and had no immunity in the United Kingdom. The RCMP had provided the British with all the transcripts of questions they had asked. One question before immunity had been granted in Canada read: "Did you meet with or communicate in any way with representatives of the Soviet bloc intelligence services during the period 1949 to 1962, including your period of employment with NATO?"

Answer: "No, I did not."

All the attorney general had to do was to read back the accused's own statements.

"Why lie on Friday?" the attorney general demanded.

"Because these things worry me, that's why."

"Is the truth really that you didn't want to admit that you had taken the NATO documents on Friday?"

"Yes, I suppose so," came the answer.

He had nowhere to retreat. Hugo shrivelled into a contrite schoolboy. "You attack me again and again." Hugo was pleading for relief, but he got very little.

Before the noon break arrived, the defendant was mentally and physically exhausted. The defence counsel fidgeted, nervously, waiting helplessly for the embarrassment to end. The machinery of the body worked automatically, but the attorney general's assault seemed to have anaesthetized Hugo's brain. His answers grew less and less related to what was being asked.

The man in the witness box bore only a distant relationship to a functioning human being.

Sir Michael asked and answered one of the last important questions of his cross-examination himself as the prisoner attempted feebly to claim a loyalty to NATO.

"Why this sudden loyalty to NATO to stop you passing secret documents? I will tell you why. Because you were scared stiff that the Russians might denounce you, and you would do anything they asked to keep in with them."

Sir Michael drove home the inescapable conclusion: "You were a spy. Is Professor Hambleton anything else but a spy?"

Shortly after, the court rose. The next day, the prosecution and the defence consulted before the trial recommenced. Sitting in the courtroom ready to be called as witnesses for the Crown were Inspector Frank Pratt of the RCMP, Raymond George Nart, head of the Soviet section of French counter-intelligence, and Bertrand Giroux, director general of the Canadian security services. To avoid further punishment to his client the defence counsel wisely reached an agreement with the prosecution. Mr. Justice Croom-Johnson then put a question to the defendant.

"Do you wish to hear the charges against you read again?"

"Yes."

"How do you plead to the first count."

"I am guilty."

In exchange for that guilty plea, the second count, spying for the Russians from 1962 to 1979, was not pursued.

Professor Hugh George Hambleton was sentenced to ten years in jail. Sir Michael rose triumphantly. He asked that the evidence of the two witnesses from the French and Canadian security services be read into the record, which they were. The trial was over. Sir Michael should really have gone over to thank Hugo for his assistance. He had flawlessly prepared the case against himself. The documents taken from NATO a quarter of a century earlier had convicted him; information once damaging to the NATO alliance could now be found by the Russians on any library shelf. The sentence completed the strange charade directed by a political expediency and concluded by a ponderous justice.

The fantasy was complete.

There were left, however, a number of questions that Canadians might very well ask of their government. Who granted immunity to Professor Hambleton in early 1980 by a communication that the attorney general of the United Kingdom admitted to on

December 6, 1982, in the Old Bailey? The existence of this correspondence was denied by Robert Kaplan, Canadian solicitor general. Did the recommendation for immunity come from a source higher than Kaplan? And if so, from whom? If the recommendation came from below, who in the security service would make this decision? If the communication existed, what happened to it?

Furthermore, by his own admission Hugh Hambleton in 1975 was interrogated by the Yugoslavian police in Belgrade and questioned on his NATO role. The Mossad the same year were aware the Canadian was a KGB agent when he travelled to Israel. Both the Yugoslavs and the Israelis knew of this Russian link at least three years before the Canadians. It took the RCMP until 1979, acting upon intelligence received from the CIA, before they took any action. Why? No one has answered these questions.

Everywhere in the world where the trial was reported there was an impression that justice had rolled on successfully. Although Sir Michael and the intelligence services of the West acted as if they had triumphed, they had all suffered a defeat. The mentally battered, imprisoned Hugo was the real victor. His friends in the KGB were still protected, the Soviet apparatus of espionage with which he was intimately familar remained unimpaired, the exact locations of the KGB operations were unrevealed, and the true nature of Hugo's activities in the Caribbean, Central and South America were shrouded in mystery.

He had told volumes it seemed, enough to entice his prosecutors. But the deep, significant secrets may be forever hidden. Should Hugo one day decide to talk, his revelations might very well force Western security services to reassess many of their operations; although if he did this, his life would be in danger.

Then again he may have no desire to tell more than he has already. His compatriots had tormented and imprisoned him. His friends had given him the adventure, the excitement and the purpose he had always sought.

The
Prisoner

Early in January 1983 I was in London. I made an appointment to visit the firm of solicitors responsible for the defence of Hugh Hambleton. They were located in a converted shop on Horseferry Road, a working-class area in the southwest of the city. On the front window was a sign that advertised "legal aid." The solicitor in charge of the case, Edward Wein, agreed to see me, although it was only after some difficulty that he accepted my phone call. We arranged to meet at five o'clock that same afternoon.

Mr. Wein made it clear immediately after I entered his office that he had been approached by others interested in the Hambleton affair, and warned he was not prepared to divulge any information.

"I have been offered money from many people to give them the story. You are only one of many who are interested."

I told Mr. Wein I had not come to offer anything but was mainly curious about someone I knew and his sad ending. I was undecided whether I would write anything. He could help me if he wished. Although he talked volubly, his hostility increased. At last he agreed to answer any questions I put in writing, provided that his client consented. Later, when Hugo gave his written permission, Wein still refused to cooperate.

By this time I had received a half-dozen letters from Hugo, and I had been granted permission to visit him in prison, only to have that permission suddenly rescinded. Through various appeals on my behalf, the Home Office finally agreed to allow me to see my old friend.

On January 20, 1983, from the cold, damp cavern of London's St. Pancras station I caught the morning train north to Leicestershire.

Market Harborough rose unexpectedly in the midst of the bleak English countryside, a typical Midland community of grimy, stained, stone buildings that began and ended nowhere in particular. One main street wound aimlessly into the town square, passed rows of boarded shop windows, then swung out again into the barren fields.

My visit to the prisoner at Gartree was scheduled for two o'clock. A car-hire firm would take me to the prison. Since I had ample time, I settled down in the White Swan Hotel for lunch. Off the dining room the bar overflowed with local businessmen who regarded me distantly, warily, as an obvious stranger who had come to town. Strangers usually came to Gartree for a single reason: to visit the high-security prison just outside its boundaries. The prisoners incarcerated at Gartree were all special cases, some of them celebrated. Unlike most other prisons, it did not suffer from overcrowding.

When I finished lunch, it was time to depart. It took only a few minutes to leave behind the last buildings of the town. The road from the town to Gartree had been travelled many times by the driver for other visitors before me. Extremely discreet, he sought no information of my mission, and I volunteered none as we turned down a small country lane and approached the high stone walls of this massive prison fortress. All that was needed was the moat, the raised drawbridge and the iron portcullis to turn Gartree into a feudal castle. Along the outside wall I could see a large Alsatian guard dog patrolling the grounds with its master. My driver, not very anxious to be seen loitering near these inhospitable premises, departed the instant he dropped me at the doorway to the office. After the visit he would pick me up and drive me the thirty miles to Leicester to catch the London Express.

The prison stands alone in the midst of hundreds of acres of empty, flat countryside. From the guard towers one has an uninterrupted view for many miles in all directions. The surroundings are intimidating. With little encouragement I would have been prepared to turn around and go home. But that was now impossible. I was irrevocably committed. My limousine was speeding away in a small dark dust cloud up the country lane beyond any hope of recall.

The entrance to the office built alongside the high prison wall was through a thick metal door, the upper part of which was made of heavy bullet-proof glass. A uniformed guard stood just within the entrance, following my approach with his eyes. Once inside the cramped office I was asked to identify myself. More guards waited behind a bullet-proof glass wicket with a narrow slit through which my documents could be presented. I explained that I had no documents, since my visit, originally granted and then denied, had had to be hurriedly reinstated by special authority from the Home Office. A high official had been good enough to vouch for me and forego the long period normally required for the security check, but there had been no time to prepare a written order. However, I noticed my name was listed on the visitors' docket.

I noticed one other visitor in the room. He was a middle-aged man with sad eyes, dressed in an open-necked shirt and a worn blue ski jacket. He faced me, sitting opposite on a wooden bench. He must surely be, I thought, a father of one of the inmates. I returned his friendly nod but neither of us spoke. Behind our smiles was the silent strained embarrassment of two people meeting in a forbidden place.

A loud buzzer sounded abrasively, then a massive steel door swung slowly open, revealing another guard who called my name and bade me follow. We entered a large, well-illuminated waiting room cut off at either end by more steel doors. A number of men, women and children were already sitting on simple wooden chairs at small tables across from the persons they had come to see. The inmates were clearly identified by their drab, faded blue trousers and similar grey open-necked shirts. But I could not observe my friend Hugo anywhere.

I was led alone to the far corner of the big room into a tiny cubicle that adjoined the door to the cells. Inside were three chairs, one on either side of a small wooden table with a third close by. The enclosure effectively isolated me from everyone else in the big room.

A single sound had echoed and re-echoed in my ears since I had come into the prison: the constant clanging of steel doors from far and near that opened and shut with a jarring dissonance that made me decidedly uncomfortable.

The far door of the cubicle opened without warning. But the prisoner did not enter. Instead, a tall gentleman of military bearing stood in the doorway. He had short-cropped hair and a neatly trimmed moustache and wore a brown canvas jacket. He introduced himself as the deputy governor; in his hand he carried a single sheet of paper which he asked me to read and sign if I agreed with the contents. Because of the nature of his offence, prisoner Hambleton, the deputy governor explained, warranted special precautions under the Official Secrets Act. I must undertake here and now not to divulge a word communicated during my visit.

I wondered how anyone would know what we would talk about. I hardly thought there were listening devices, since there was a noticeable lack of sophistication about this prison fortress. Perhaps I would not be left alone with the prisoner. I quickly read two faded paragraphs typed on a sheet of cheap paper.

The deputy governor was quite friendly. His wife's family lived in Aurora, Ontario, not far from Toronto, which he visited yearly. We exchanged a few more pleasantries, then he disappeared with his signed sheet of paper without a further word. A few moments later a cell door close by clanged shut. The prisoner, accompanied by a burly jail warden, entered the cubicle. Hugo had lost weight since I had last seen him. He was greyer than I remembered, and more pallid. But he gripped my hand firmly and with a hearty burst of energy laughed as if he were somewhere else. What a splendid performance.

The guard, blank-faced, expressionless, sank into his chair and pretended to be invisible. I removed my notebook to keep some details of the meeting for my personal record. No objections were raised. The guard, as if to show his total indifference, buried his nose in his own small notebook, making a few entries. Was all this pretence? The guard's name, I learned, was Conlan.

Hugo found the prison company pleasant compared to those with whom he had been associated outside the prison walls. He acted almost relieved to be where he was, freed from all responsibility and protected from the relentless eyes and ears of the press and his inquisitors. The monastic conditions of prison life, providing the basic necessities of existence, fitted his own style of living. Also he seemed pleased to be learning a machinist's trade. The carefully tooled metal parts he made on his lathe conformed to the perfectionist quality in the character of the man himself.

For over two hours I asked Hugo every conceivable question that had been on my mind since his trial. On this day he was guarded, as he had to be. But I knew him well enough to decipher the content of what he wished to communicate. What Hugo said answered one of the last questions that lay in my mind. Since I am forbidden to relate our conversation lest I contravene the Official Secrets Act, and since there is strong evidence that the guard recorded what was said, Hugo's secrets have been revealed in other ways in this book. In his six letters to me from prison prior to this visit, he had intimated as much as a man could say.

Adding to those letters what he told me in Quebec and interpreting what he tried to say again in my prison visit, the story became as complete as it could be—without Hugo ever revealing all the truth.

A volunteer woman helper poked her head into the room. Conlan snapped suddenly to life.

"Tea," he said in his thick working-class Belfast accent. "You can buy it for the prisoner, but he can't buy any for you."

"I'll buy," I said amicably. Hugo agreed, but the guard refused my hospitality. It was the humblest of bribes.

The volunteer wheeled in a tea trolley, poured two mugs of warm tea, and left some hard chocolate biscuits wrapped in cellophane on the table. She left without looking at either me or the prisoner.

I turned to Hugo once more, but the fidgeting Conlan warned my visiting time was up. My personal quest was now coming to a close at last, after many long months.

"Canadians should at least be permitted to prosecute their own spies, Hugo. We don't need the British to do that for us," I said lightly.

"Well, we got our Constitution back," he grinned. "That's something."

"Can I send you anything?" I offered. "I left a yachting magazine with the guard at the entrance. I thought it might interest you."

Hugo thanked me laconically. He didn't need anything. His needs at the best of times were minimal. "My sister mails me everything I need. I've requested some books on Spain. Everything here is not to my liking, but it could be worse."

The chocolate biscuits remained untouched on the table. The guard indicated that Hugo could take them, and he put them in his pocket as Conlan pointed back in the direction of the cells.

I said my brief good-bye, and we shook hands quickly. The occasion was not terribly solemn, but I knew I would probably not be seeing Hugo again. Followed by his guard, the prisoner went out through the steel door to be locked up in his steel cage.

In the big waiting room I exchanged another nod with the middle-aged man in the blue ski jacket whom I had seen when I arrived. He sat across one of the small tables from a slim, pallid youth with dyed yellow hair and bad teeth. I walked quickly, since I was not anxious to remain inside this depressing institution a moment longer than I had to. The threat of confinement touched everyone who entered.

I waited impatiently for the door to the outside world to open.

As it did, I stepped over the threshold with relief. The big Alsatian still patrolled the grounds. My car came down the winding lane a little ahead of time. No sooner had I stepped into the vehicle and closed the door than the driver sped off again. Scarcely a second was lost.

"It's not good to be seen loitering around here, governor. Not this prison," he said.

Out on the main road to Leicester, we raced to catch the five o'clock train to London. My driver was quite talkative after he learned I was from Canada. He informed me that Irish Republican gunmen were kept at Gartree along with the notorious Kray twins, the former chiefs of the biggest crime syndicate in England.

"Then there is this big spy, Hambleton," he said.

The prisoner I met at Gartree that afternoon was not the Hugh Hambleton I knew. He appeared the same on the surface, talked the same as I remembered and might have acted the same from time to time. But he had been emptied of all emotion and feeling. Only the shell was left.

After my visit to Gartree all communication ceased. There were no more letters from Hugo. But on February 24 of that same year I received a letter from Hugo's law firm on Horseferry Road. The signature was in the name of the firm. Only one sentence is relevant. It read:

> *Mr. Hambleton confirmed to us*
> *that he did not know you*
> *as you informed us he did.*

As I write this, Bessie Hambleton is alive at ninety-five, outraged by the infirmities of old age, rebelling against the afflictions that have imprisoned her in her home on Ruskin Avenue. She is silent about the one great disappointment of her life. The golden future for her son is no more than a dream.